DEAD THEOLOGIANS SOCIETY

Founded in 1997, the youth and young adult apostolate, Dead Theologians Society, through the lives of the saints, inspires young people to grow in holiness and in the imitation of Christ. A special charism of the Dead Theologians Society is to pray for the Souls in Purgatory.

A unique aspect of the apostolate is, at every Dead Theologians Society meeting, young people – members of the Church Militant, learn about the lives of, and ask for the intercession of, the Saints - the Church Triumphant, while praying for the Souls in Purgatory – the Church Suffering, thereby involving the 'entire family' of the Church.

In 2015, the Dead Theologians Society received canonical standing as a Private Association of the Faithful and is headquartered in the Diocese of Madison, Wisconsin, USA.

This beautifully presented book is a wonderful collection of quotes of saints from both recent and ancient times. The saints form that *"great cloud of witnesses,"* who spur us on to continue to walk with God on the journey of life. (Hebrews 12:1).

In December 2019 Pope Francis told a group in Rome that, *"Saints are models and guides of Christian life, but they are not unreachable human beings"*. In fact, he said, *"they are people who have experienced the daily toil of existence with its successes and failures, finding in the Lord the strength to always get up and continue the journey."* Saints inspire us and God knows we need inspiration.

I heartily congratulate Eddie Cotter on the publication of this valuable book. May the wisdom of these men and women of faith who knew what is was to suffer and yet to be joyful through it all help you in whatever situation you find yourself.

May this book provide you with a daily allowance of spiritual light to carry out God's will and help you struggle on to live with joy in the presence of God each day, seeing things from a supernatural point of view and bringing God's love and mercy to those you meet.

His Grace The Most Reverend Alphonsus Cullinan

Bishop of Waterford and Lismore, Ireland

From the Author

Many years ago, I read a quote from St. John Vianney which said, *"Anger never travels alone. It is always accompanied by plenty of other sins."* The wisdom contained in that short quote has provided for me a lifetime of inspiration and, at times, the needed reminder!

It inspired me to search for life-changing wisdom from the treasury of our Saints, that could be easily imparted to a multitude of people.

Please God, these great *"one-liners"* from the Saints, will assist you in this life, and help you to grow in holiness and ultimately reach Heaven.

Eddie Cotter, Jr.

Founder, Dead Theologians Society

JANUARY
THE HOLY NAME OF JESUS

Adoration of the Name of Jesus
by Juan de Roelas (1605)

Wisdom & Inspiration from the Saints for

JANUARY

JANUARY 01

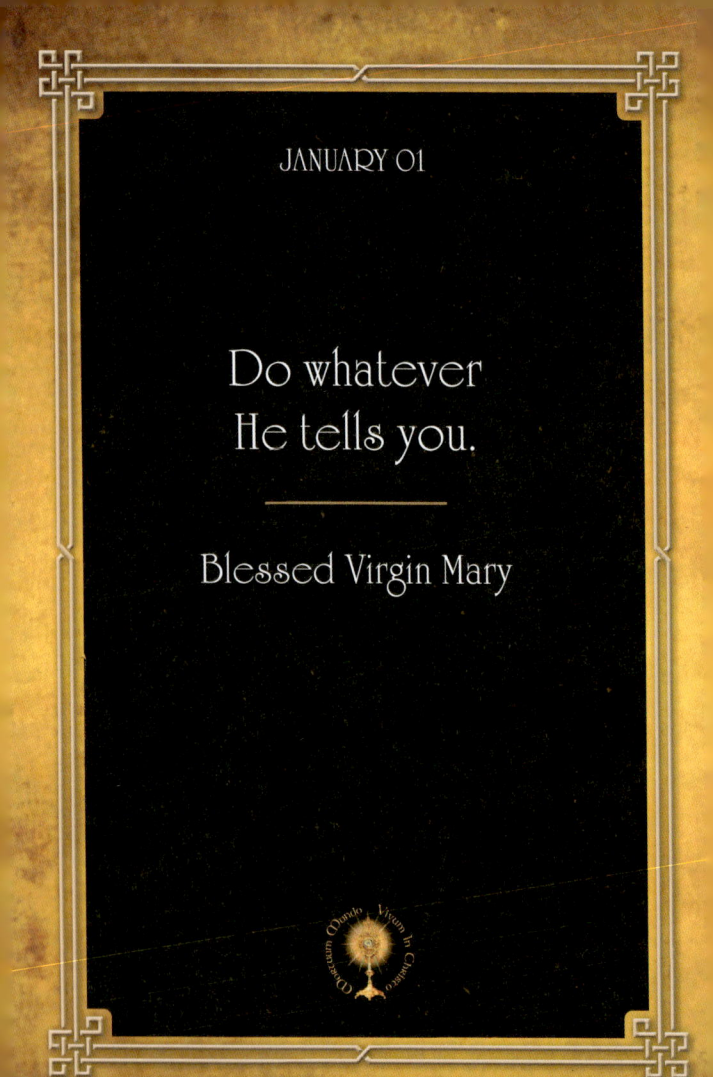

Do whatever
He tells you.

Blessed Virgin Mary

JANUARY 02

When you sit down to eat... pray.

Saint Basil the Great

JANUARY 03

We only need to open our eyes to see the gifts that abound all around us.

―――

Saint Genevieve

JANUARY 04

Cheerfulness prepares a glorious mind for all the noblest acts.

Saint Elizabeth Ann Seton

JANUARY 05

A man must always be ready, for death comes when and where God wills it.

———

Saint John Neumann

JANUARY 06

When you say
the Our Father,
God's ear is next
to your lips.

Saint Andre Bessette

JANUARY 07

The preacher of God's truth has told us, that all who want to live righteously, in Christ, will suffer persecution.

Saint Raymond of Penafort

JANUARY 08

We therefore grossly deceive ourselves in not allotting more time to the study of divine truths.

———

Saint Apollinaris

JANUARY 09

Do not pray
for easy lives, pray
to be stronger.

———

Blessed Solanus Casey

JANUARY 10

I have vowed to my God to teach the heathen, though I be despised by some.

———

Saint Patrick

JANUARY 11

Our friend becomes an enemy if he would cause us to sin.

———

Saint Francis de Sales

JANUARY 12

Prayer ought to carry out into our thoughts, our words, and our actions.

Saint Marguerite Bourgeoys

JANUARY 13

No matter how sinful one may have been, if he has devotion to Mary, it is impossible that he be lost.

———

Saint Hilary of Poitiers

JANUARY 14

I exhort you earnestly never to give way to anger; and never, under any pretext whatever, let it effect an entrance into your heart.

Saint Francis de Sales

JANUARY 15

Three things God most detests: a scowling face, obstinacy in wrongdoing, and too great a confidence in the power of money.

Saint Ita of Ireland

JANUARY 16

The Judge will show mercy in proportion as we show it.

Saint Elizabeth Ann Seton

JANUARY 17

He (the Devil) runs away when we make the sign of the cross.

Saint Anthony the Abbot

JANUARY 18

Prudence is knowing what to want and what not to want.

Saint Thomas Aquinas

JANUARY 19

It is most certain that, as we share here below in the prayers of one another, so these same prayers and good works profit the souls in Purgatory, who can be helped by them.

Saint Francis de Sales

JANUARY 20

The devil strains every nerve to secure the souls which belong to Christ.

―――

Saint Sebastian

JANUARY 21

You may stain your sword with my blood, but you will never be able to profane my body, consecrated to Christ.

———

Saint Agnes

JANUARY 22

In all He did from the Incarnation to the Cross, the end Jesus Christ had in mind was the gift of the Eucharist, his personal and corporal union with each Christian through Communion.

Saint Peter Julian Eymard

JANUARY 23

I am not afraid of any disease; hence, it would be my greatest delight to minister to the abandoned lepers.

Saint Marianne Cope

JANUARY 24

Nothing is so strong as gentleness, nothing so gentle as real strength.

———

Saint Francis de Sales

JANUARY 25

That which comes from Satan begins in calmness and ends in storm, indifference and apathy.

Saint Padre Pio

JANUARY 26

If you think I will swear by the genius of Caesar, then you don't know who I am.

Saint Polycarp

JANUARY 27

To destroy the fetus is worse than murder, for the one who does this does not take away life that has already been born, but prevents it from being born.

Saint John Chrysostom

JANUARY 28

When the devil is called the God of this world, it is not because he made it, but because we serve him with our worldliness.

Saint Thomas Aquinas

JANUARY 29

Look back, I beseech thee, and come to Christ, since you labor and are bent down with your huge burden, and He, as He has said, will give you rest.

Saint Gildas the Wise

JANUARY 30

Trust all things to Jesus in the Blessed Sacrament and to Mary, Help of Christians and you will see what miracles are.

Saint John Bosco

JANUARY 31

The power of evil men lives on the cowardice of the good.

Saint John Bosco

Dead Theologians
Society was founded
in 1997.

FEBRUARY
THE HOLY FAMILY

The Holy Family
by Bartolomé Esteban Murillo

Wisdom & Inspiration from the Saints for

FEBRUARY

FEBRUARY 01

It is impossible for a man to be freed from the habit of sin before he hates it, just as it is impossible to receive forgiveness before confessing his trespass.

Saint Ignatius of Antioch

FEBRUARY 02

It is a virtue and a prize to put up with insults for the sake of God.

Saint Brigid of Kildare

FEBRUARY 03

If I were worthy of such a favor from my God, I would ask that He grant me this one miracle: that by His grace He would make me a good man.

Saint Ansgar

FEBRUARY 04

Virgin Mother, because I am thy servant, I will unceasingly serve thee.

Saint Andrew Corsini

FEBRUARY 05

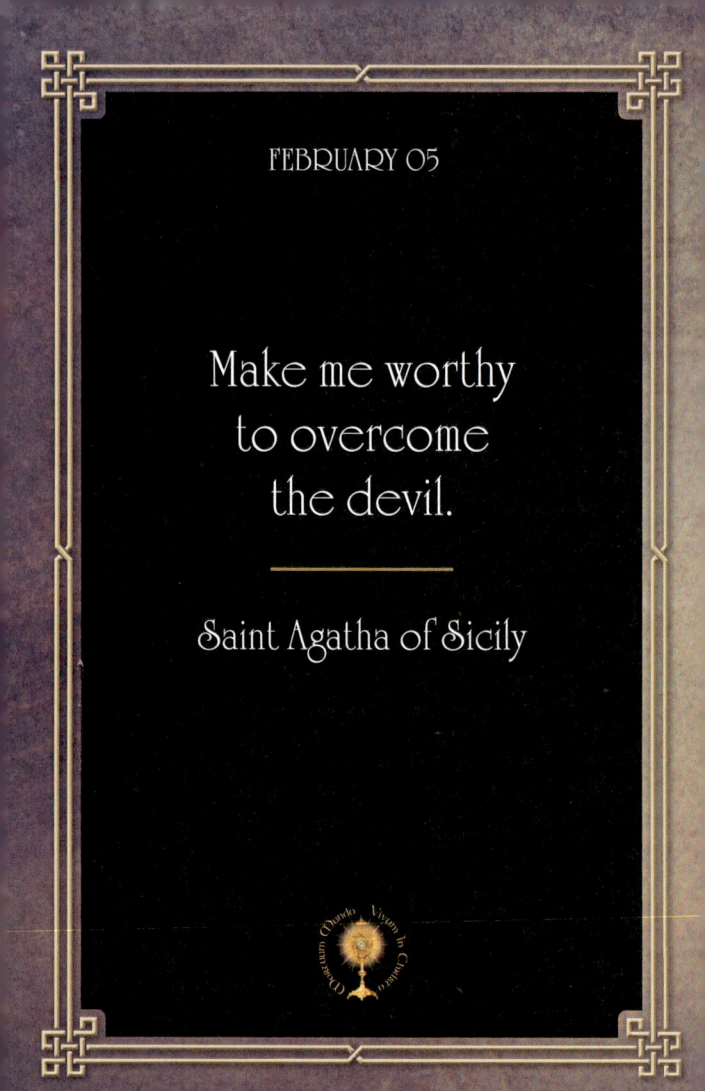

Make me worthy to overcome the devil.

Saint Agatha of Sicily

FEBRUARY 06

Ask Christ
to help you to
become happy.

Saint Paul Miki

FEBRUARY 07

Watch your thoughts like a good fisherman watching for fish.

Saint Romuald

FEBRUARY 08

The best thing for us is not what we consider best, but what the Lord wants of us.

Saint Josephine Bakhita

FEBRUARY 09

As two pieces of wax fused together make one, so he who receives Holy Communion is so united with Christ that Christ is in him and he is in Christ.

———

Saint Cyril of Alexandria

FEBRUARY 10

If men knew the peace good Religious enjoy, the whole world would become a monastery.

Saint Scholastica

FEBRUARY 11

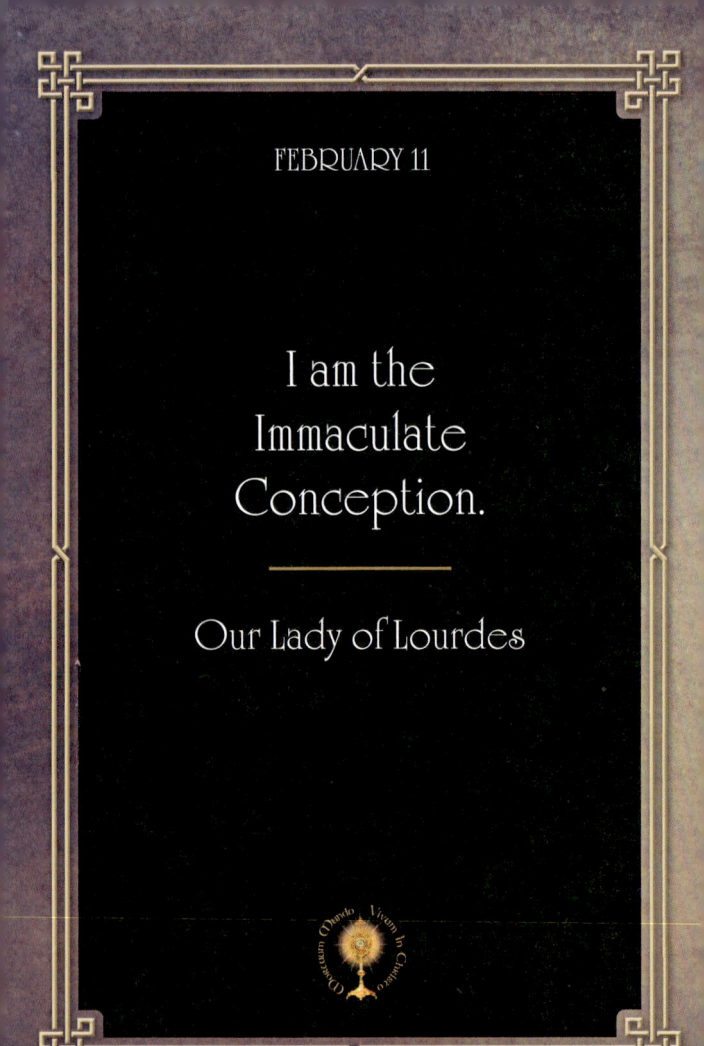

I am the Immaculate Conception.

Our Lady of Lourdes

FEBRUARY 12

Religion is
the science of
saving souls.

Blessed Solanus Casey

FEBRUARY 13

God loves us more than we love ourselves, and takes more care of us than we could take care of ourselves.

―――

Saint Catherine de Ricci

FEBRUARY 14

Neither backbite, nor lend a willing ear to backbiters; but rather be prompt to prayer.

―――

Saint Cyril of Jerusalem

FEBRUARY 15

A man who leans on God is immovable and cannot be overthrown.

―――

Saint Claude
de la Colombiere

FEBRUARY 16

After the love which we owe Jesus Christ, we must give the chief place in our heart to the love of His mother Mary.

Saint Alphonsus Liguori

FEBRUARY 17

This is how we can repay such blessings, when our lives change and we come to know God, to praise and bear witness to His great wonders before every nation under heaven.

Saint Patrick

FEBRUARY 18

My job is to inform,
not to convince.

Saint Bernadette
Soubirous

FEBRUARY 19

You are my Mother, the Mother of Mercy, and the consolation for the souls in Purgatory.

Saint Bridget to
Our Lady

FEBRUARY 20

If men only knew what eternity is, they would do everything in their power to change their lives.

―――

Saint Jacinta Marto

FEBRUARY 21

Nobody can fight properly or boldly for the faith if he clings to the fear of being stripped of earthly possessions.

Saint Peter Damian

FEBRUARY 22

The fire of Purgatory is the same as the fire of Hell; the difference between them is that the fire of Purgatory is not everlasting.

―――

Saint John Vianney

FEBRUARY 23

When you have
the opportunity
to do good,
do not let it go by.

Saint Polycarp

FEBRUARY 24

God gives us
health so that we may
serve the sick.

Blessed Pier
Giorgio Frassati

FEBRUARY 25

As we see bread and wine with our bodily eyes, let us see and firmly believe that it is the holy Body and Blood, true and living.

Saint Francis of Assisi

FEBRUARY 26

Two very bad things are ill-will and unbelief, both of which are contrary to righteousness; for ill-will is opposed to charity, and unbelief to faith; just as in the same way as bitterness is opposed to sweetness, darkness to light, evil to good, death to life, falsehood to truth.

Saint Alexander

FEBRUARY 27

Fidelity in little things, must be the basic rule in striving for holiness.

Saint Gabriel of
Our Lady of Sorrows

FEBRUARY 28

The privilege of our Church is such that it is never stronger than when it is attacked, never better known than when it is accused, never more powerful than when it appears forsaken.

Saint Hilary of Poitiers

MARCH
SAINT JOSEPH

Saint Joseph and the Christ Child
by Bartolomé Esteban Murillo (1666)

Wisdom & Inspiration from the Saints for

MARCH

MARCH 01

Be joyful,
keep your faith and
your creed.

Saint David

MARCH 02

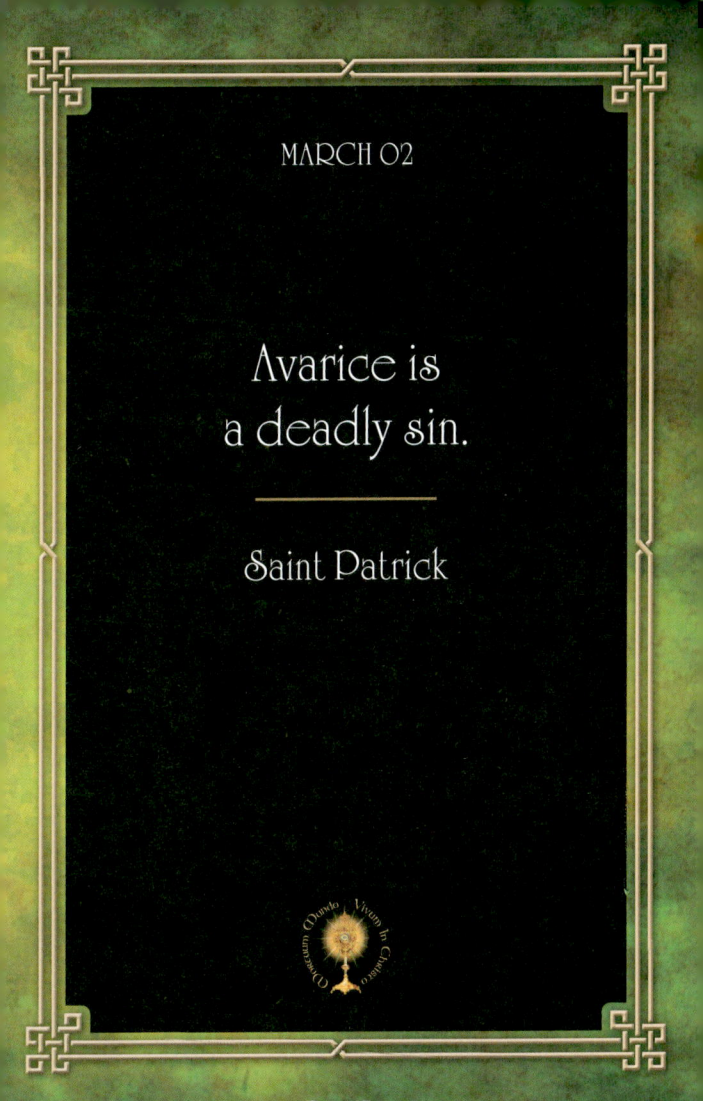

Avarice is a deadly sin.

Saint Patrick

MARCH 03

My sweetest joy is
to be in the presence
of Jesus in the
Holy Sacrament.

Saint Katharine Drexel

MARCH 04

Were we only to correspond to God's graces, continually being showered down on everyone of us, we would be able to pass from being great sinners one day to being great saints the next.

Blessed Solanus Casey

MARCH 05

It is a great wisdom to know how to be silent and to look at neither the remarks, nor the deeds, nor the lives of others.

Saint John Joseph of the Cross

MARCH 06

If through human weakness we fail, we must always without delay arise again by means of holy penance, and give our attention to leading a good life and to dying a holy death.

Saint Colette

MARCH 07

If the highest aim of a captain were to preserve his ship, he would keep it in port forever.

───

Saint Thomas Aquinas

MARCH 08

The first (virtue) is faith, believing all that holy mother church believes and holds, keeping and putting into practice what she commands.

Saint John of God

MARCH 09

A married woman must when called upon, leave her devotions to God at the altar to find Him in her household affairs

---

Saint Frances of Rome

MARCH 10

Before I was humiliated, I was like a stone that lies deep in mud, and He who is mighty came and, in His compassion, raised me up and exalted me very high and placed me on the top of the wall.

Saint Patrick

MARCH 11

The sacrifice most pleasing to God is contrition of heart.

Saint Eulogius

MARCH 12

If you aspire to the heights of real honor, strive to reach the kingdom of Heaven.

―――――

Saint Gregory the Great

MARCH 13

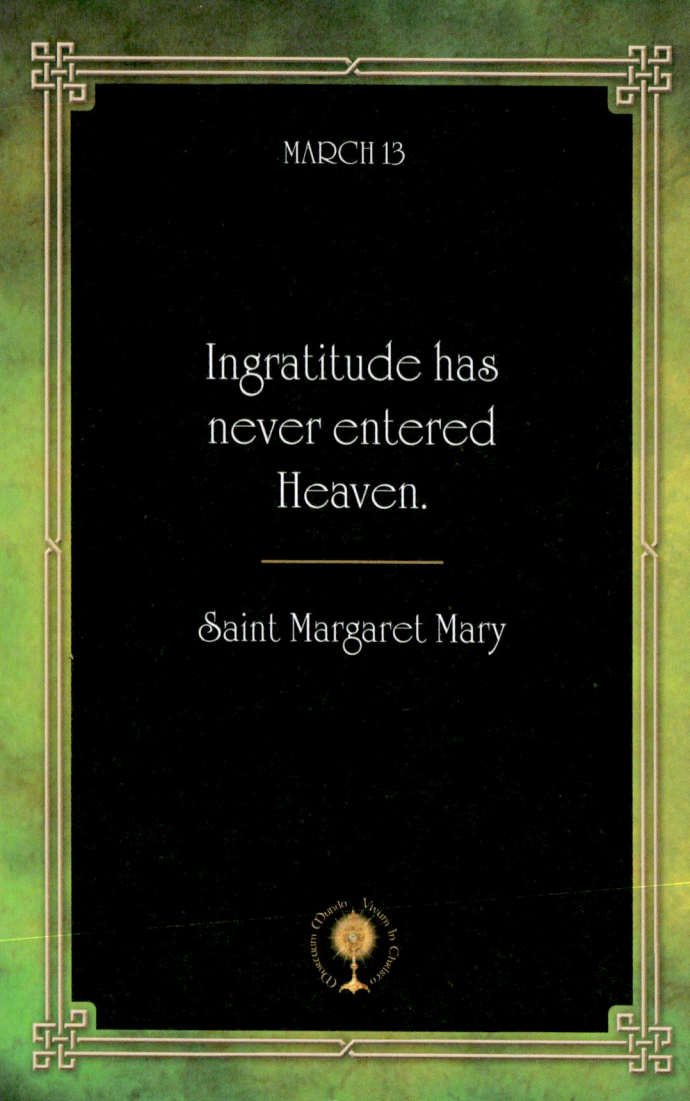

Ingratitude has never entered Heaven.

Saint Margaret Mary

MARCH 14

We must say many prayers for the souls of the faithful departed, for one must be so pure to enter Heaven.

Saint John Vianney

MARCH 15

Love the poor, honor them, my children, as you would honor Christ Himself.

Saint Louise de Marillac

MARCH 16

There is no one else on earth or in Heaven that God Himself loves as He loves His ever Virgin Immaculate Mother and wishes her to be known and loved.

———

Blessed Solanus Casey

MARCH 17

I am certain in
my heart, that all that
I am, I have received
from God.

———

Saint Patrick

MARCH 18

Since Christ Himself said, "This is My Body" who shall dare to doubt that It is His Body.

———

Saint Cyril of Jerusalem

MARCH 19

I am not capable of doing big things, but I want to do everything, even the smallest things, for the greater glory of God.

Saint Dominic Savio

MARCH 20

I care only about doing the will of God, doing it well, in the present moment.

Blessed Chiara
Luce Badano

MARCH 21

Prefer nothing, absolutely nothing, to the love of Christ.

Saint Benedict

MARCH 22

Each state of life has its special duties; by their accomplishments one may find happiness.

Saint Nicholas of Flue

MARCH 23

Christ said,
"I am the Truth",
He did not say,
"I am the custom."

———

Saint Turibius

MARCH 24

Let the truth be your light… proclaim it…but with a certain congeniality.

———

Saint Catherine of Sweden

MARCH 25

I ground my faith upon Jesus Christ, and by Him I steadfastly believe to be saved, as is taught in the Catholic Church through all Christendom, and promised to remain with her unto the world's end, and hell gates shall not prevail against it.

Saint Margaret Clitherow

MARCH 26

To live without faith, without a heritage to defend, without battling constantly for truth, is not to live but to 'get along'; we must never just 'get along'.

Blessed Pier Giorgio Frassati

MARCH 27

When thoughts are choking me like so many thorns, I enter the church, the hospital of souls.

───────

Saint John Damascene

MARCH 28

Glow with the brightness that comes from the good example of a praiseworthy and blameless life.

―――

Saint John of Capistrano

MARCH 29

Control your appetites before they control you.

Saint John Climacus

MARCH 30

Humility is the only thing that no devil can imitate.

Saint John Climacus

MARCH 31

Do not think of the bread and wine as mere bread and wine for they constitute the body and blood of Christ by the Lord's own declaration.

Saint Cyril of Jerusalem

Dead Theologians Society is Entrusted to Our Lady –

Queen of All Saints.

APRIL
THE BLESSED SACRAMENT

Adoration of the Blessed Sacrament
by Anthony Richter (1756)

Wisdom & Inspiration from the Saints for

APRIL

APRIL 01

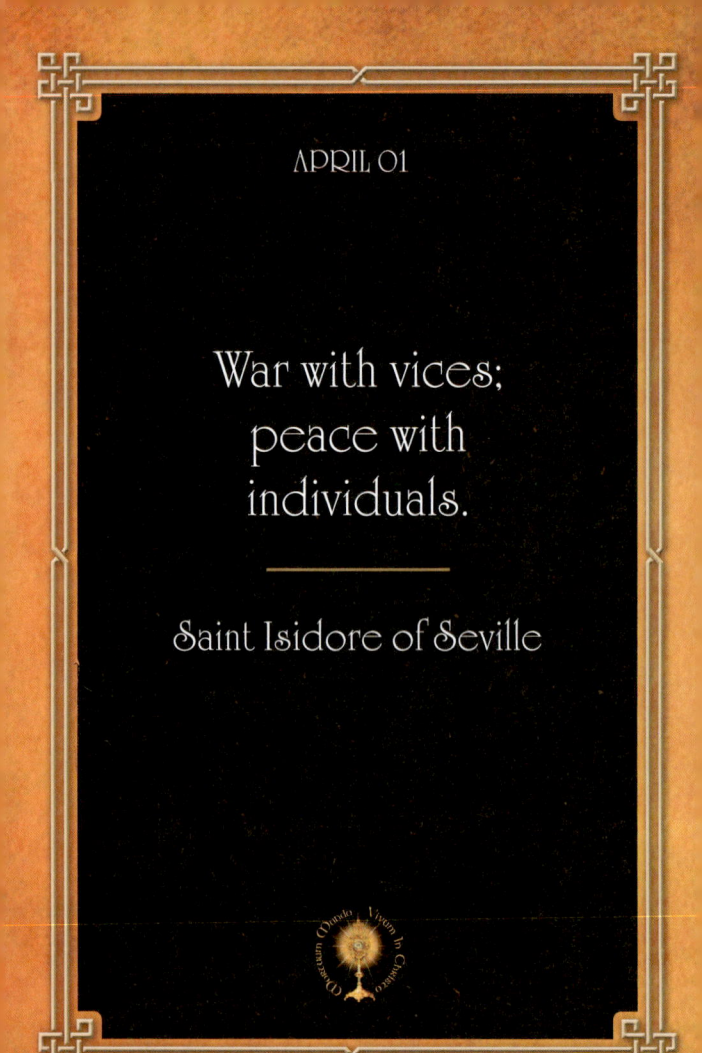

War with vices; peace with individuals.

Saint Isidore of Seville

APRIL 02

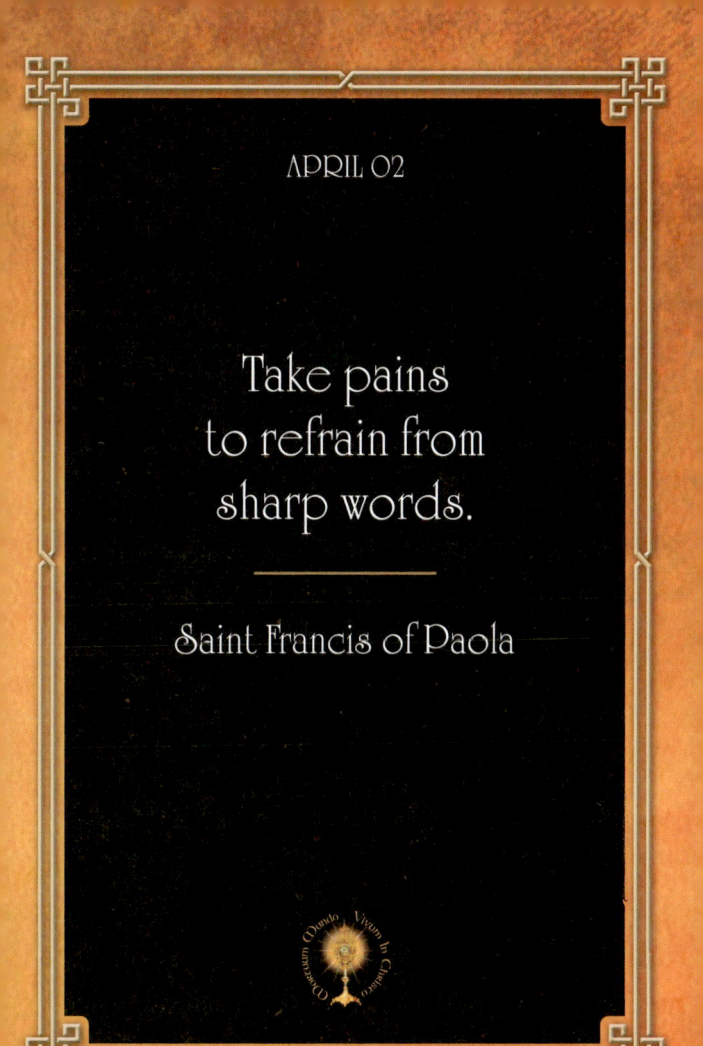

Take pains
to refrain from
sharp words.

Saint Francis of Paola

APRIL 03

Lord Jesus Christ, I thank you for all the blessings You have given me, and for all the sufferings and shame You endured for me.

Saint Richard of Chichester

APRIL 04

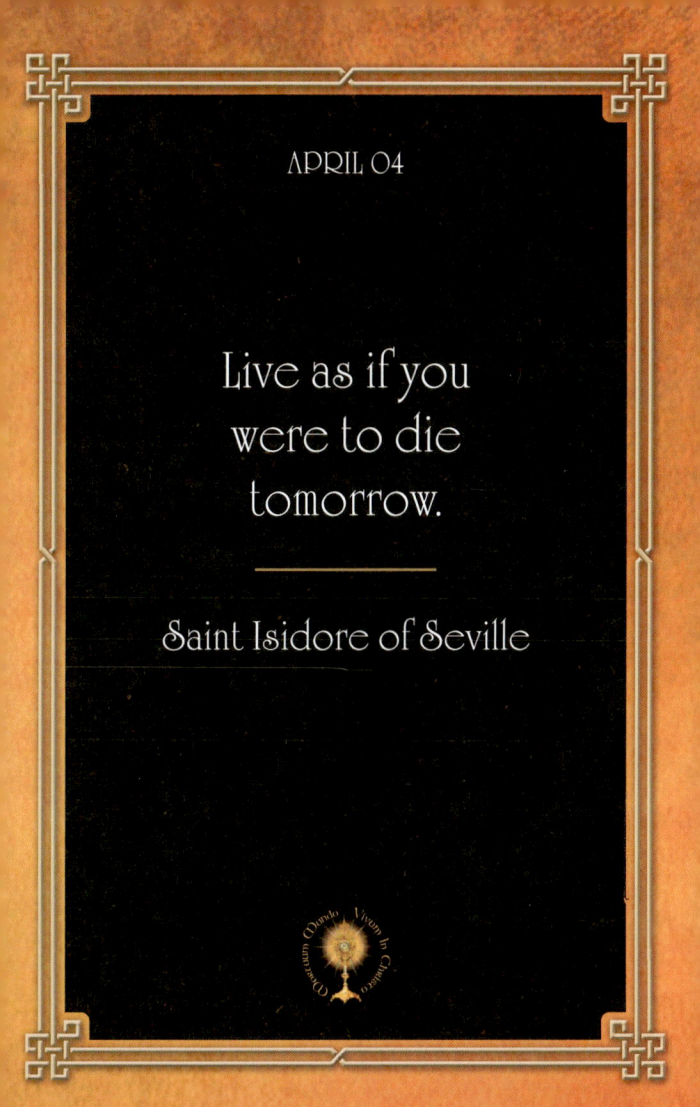

Live as if you were to die tomorrow.

Saint Isidore of Seville

APRIL 05

If you truly want to help the soul of your neighbor, you should approach God first with all your heart.

Saint Vincent Ferrer

APRIL 06

A great safeguard is the entire faith, the true faith, in which neither anything whatever can be added by anyone nor anything taken away; for unless faith be one, it is not the faith.

———

Saint Leo the Great

APRIL 07

Your face should be happy, showing gentleness and respect.

Saint John Baptist
de la Salle

APRIL 08

Very courageous souls are needed for the service of the good God.

Saint Julie Billiart

APRIL 09

Be as blind to the faults of your neighbor as possible, trying at least to attribute a good intention to their actions.

Blessed Solanus Casey

APRIL 10

If you invoke the name of the Blessed Virgin when you are tempted, She will come at once to your help, and Satan will leave you.

Saint John Vianney

APRIL 11

If you really want to learn to love Jesus, learn to suffer, because suffering teaches you to love.

———

Saint Gemma Galgani

APRIL 12

Faith enables us to bear the thorns with which our life is woven.

Blessed Pier Giorgio Frassati

APRIL 13

To save the souls of poor sinners, God wishes to establish devotion to My Immaculate Heart throughout the world.

Our Lady of Fatima

APRIL 14

You are afraid to suffer, but it were better to thank God for it, since the more you undergo down here, the less you will endure above.

Saint Lydwine

APRIL 15

We never give more honor to Jesus than when we honor His mother, and we honor Her simply and solely to honor Him all the more perfectly.

Saint Louis Marie de Montfort

APRIL 16

Oh Jesus, I would rather die a thousand deaths than to be unfaithful to you!

Saint Bernadette Soubirous

APRIL 17

Let every tongue confess that Jesus Christ, in whom we believe and whom we await to come back to us in the near future is Lord and God.

―――――

Saint Patrick

APRIL 18

There is waiting for me something better; eternal life, given to the person who has lived well on earth.

―――

Saint Apollonius

APRIL 19

Men do not fear a powerful hostile army as the powers of Hell fear the name and protection of Mary.

———

Saint Bonaventure

APRIL 20

My plan of life is chiefly this: to love and suffer, always meditating upon, adoring and admiring God's unspeakable love for his lowliest creatures.

Saint Conrad of Parzham

APRIL 21

For I do not seek to understand in order that I may believe, but I believe in order that I may understand.

Saint Anselm

APRIL 22

You cannot put straight in others what is warped in yourself.

―――――

Saint Athanasius

APRIL 23

Be very careful to retain peace of heart, because Satan casts his lines in troubled waters.

Saint Paul of the Cross

APRIL 24

What are we doing in this world, and why are we here, if not to contribute to the well being of our neighbors?

Saint Euphrasia Pelletier

APRIL 25

Do not become a disciple of one who praises himself, in case you learn pride instead of humility.

Saint Mark the Ascetic

APRIL 26

In order to bring true peace back to my soul, the only way that there exists on the Earth is Confession, because Jesus awaits me with His immense heart.

Saint Gianna Molla

APRIL 27

Better that only a few Catholics should be left, staunch and sincere in their religion, than that they should, remaining many, desire as it were, to be in collusion with the Church's enemies and in conformity with the open foes of our faith.

Saint Peter Canisius

APRIL 28

Never will anyone who says his Rosary every day become a formal heretic or be led astray by the devil.

Saint Louis Marie de Montfort

APRIL 29

Be who God meant you to be and you will set the world on fire.

Saint Catherine of Siena

APRIL 30

All the evils in the world are due to lukewarm Catholics.

―――――

Pope Saint Pius V

MAY
THE BLESSED VIRGIN MARY

Madonna and Child
by Giovanni Battista Salvi da Sassoferrato (1640)

Wisdom & Inspiration from the Saints for

MAY

MAY 01

At Communion we ought to ask for the remedy of the vice to which we feel ourselves most inclined.

Philip Neri

MAY 02

If the world goes against truth, then go against the world!

Saint Athanasius

MAY 03

Self-love is like the worm that gnaws at the root & destroys not only the fruit, but even the very life of the plant.

Saint Mary Magdalen de Pazzi

MAY 04

Nothing is far from God.

Saint Monica

MAY 05

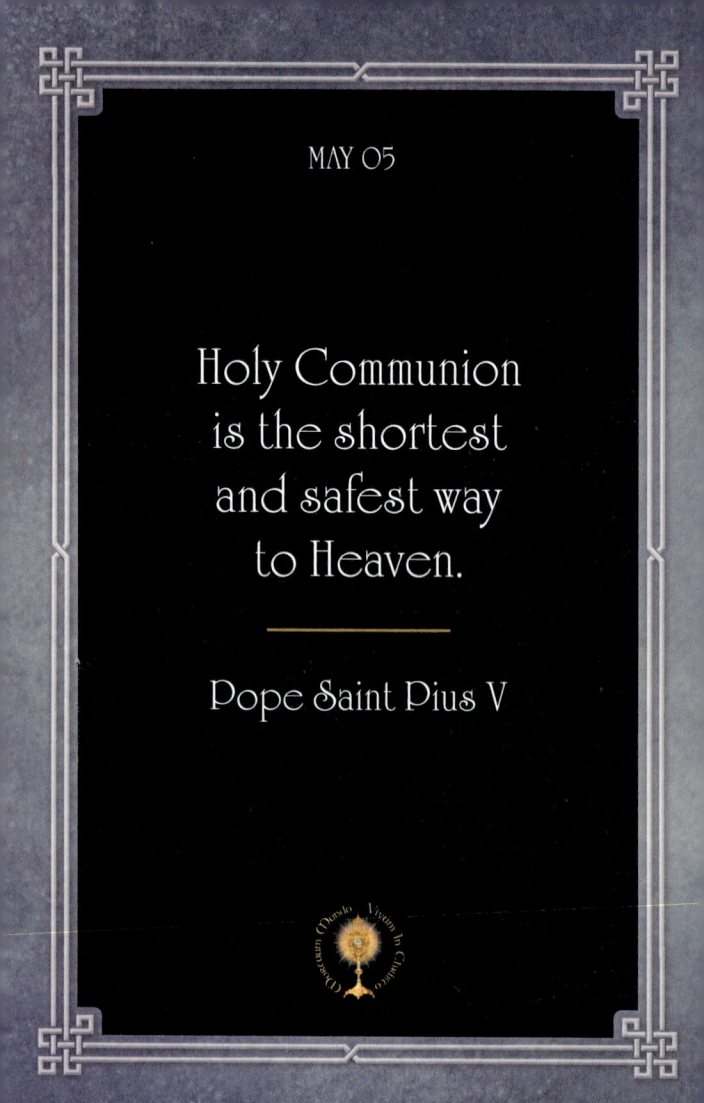

Holy Communion is the shortest and safest way to Heaven.

―

Pope Saint Pius V

MAY 06

We have no greater advocate and mediator with Christ than His Holy Mother.

Saint Robert Bellarmine

MAY 07

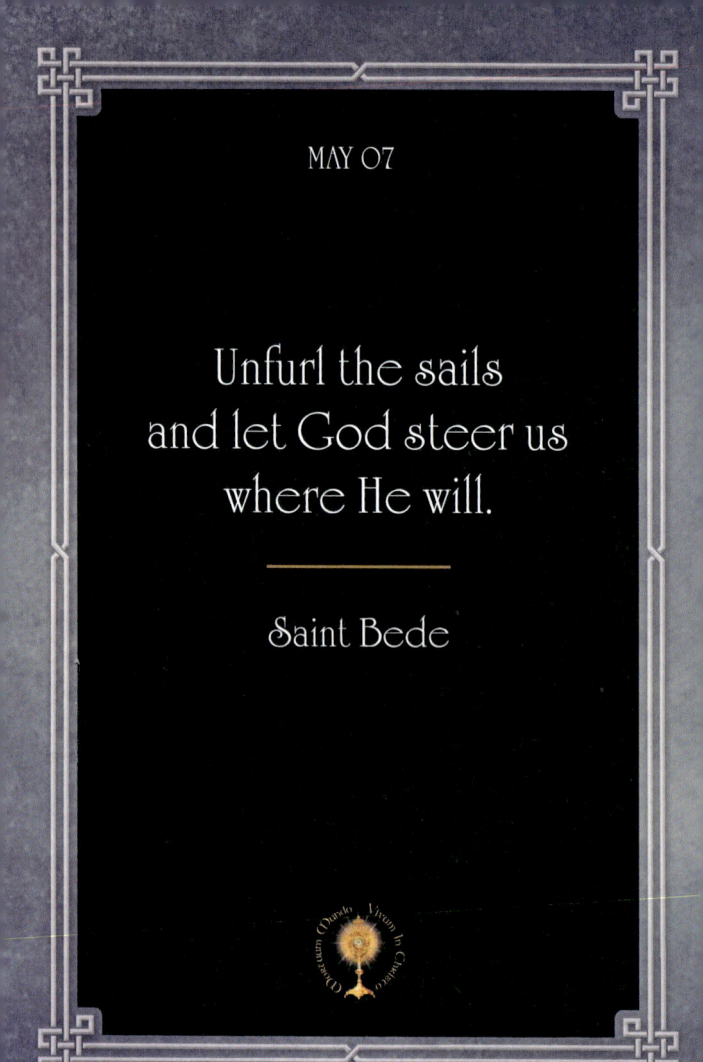

Unfurl the sails
and let God steer us
where He will.

———

Saint Bede

MAY 08

We are not in the world to follow our own will and pleasure, but to imitate the Lord.

———

Saint John Baptist de Rossi

MAY 09

May God preserve me from being rich while they are indigent, from enjoying robust health if I do not try to cure their diseases, from eating good food, clothing myself well and resting in my home if I do not share with them a piece of my bread and give them, in the measure of my abilities, part of my clothes and if I do not welcome them into my home.

Saint Gregory Nazianzen

MAY 10

I find consolation in the one and only friend who will never leave me, that is our Divine Savior in the Eucharist.

―――

Saint Damien of Molokai

MAY 11

Believe me, there is no more powerful means to obtain God's grace than to employ the intercessions of the Holy Virgin.

Saint Philip Neri

MAY 12

Whoever finds God finds everything, whoever loses God loses everything.

―――

Saint Robert Bellarmine

MAY 13

Pray, pray much and sacrifice for sinners, for many souls go to hell because there is no one to sacrifice and pray for them.

———

Our Lady of Fatima

MAY 14

Let us fix our eyes on the crucifix in every difficult moment and that gaze will renew our courage.

Saint Madeleine
Sophie Barat

MAY 15

God has
chosen you to make
Him known to
others.

———

Saint John Baptist
de la Salle

MAY 16

I will believe You for my future, chapter by chapter, until the story is written.

Saint Brendan
the Navigator

MAY 17

God is as really present in the consecrated Host as He is in the glory of Heaven.

———

Saint Paschal Baylon

MAY 18

I was no longer the centre of my life and therefore I could see God in everything.

Saint Bede

MAY 19

We hold it to be far nobler to fight for a long time for freedom of the Holy Church than to sink into a miserable and devilish servitude.

Saint Gregory VII

MAY 20

Whenever the divine favor chooses someone to receive a special grace, or to accept a lofty vocation, God adorns the person chosen with all the gifts of the Spirit needed to fulfill the task at hand.

Saint Bernardine of Siena

MAY 21

I forgive with all my heart those responsible for my death, and I ask God that the shedding of my blood serve the peace of our divided Mexico.

Saint Christopher Magallanes

MAY 22

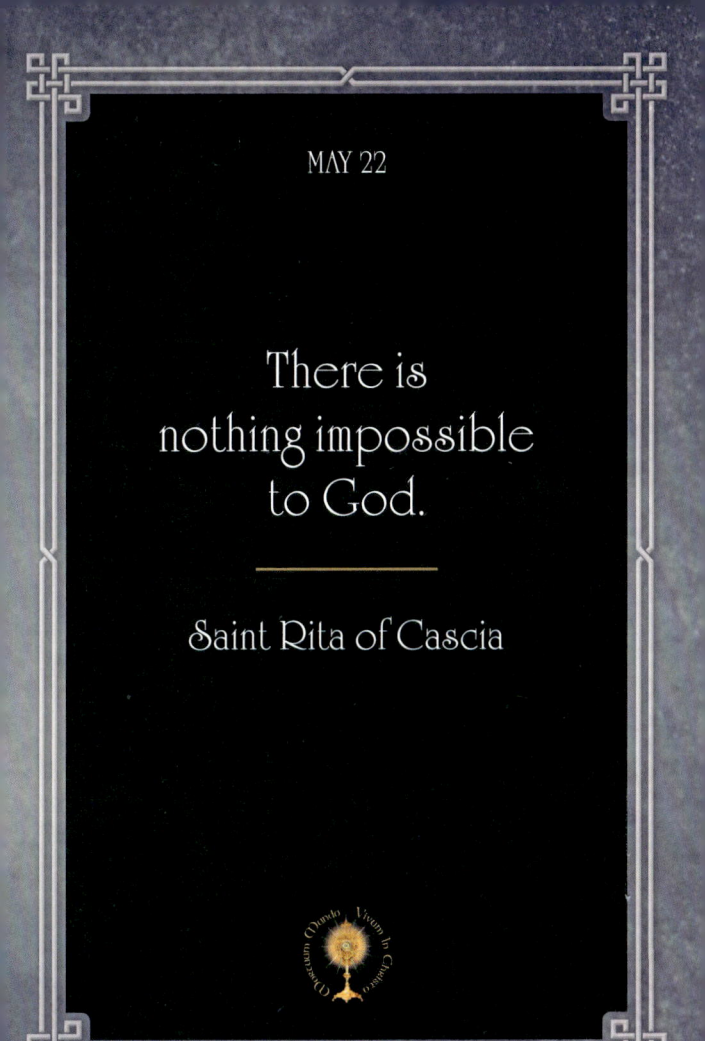

There is nothing impossible to God.

Saint Rita of Cascia

MAY 23

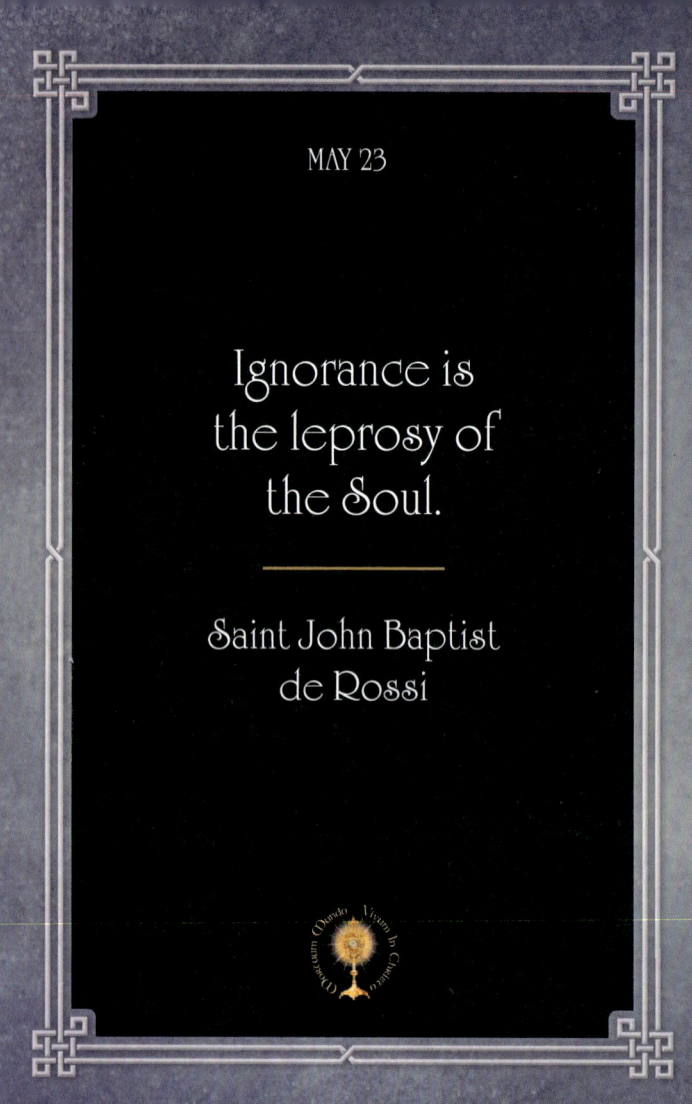

Ignorance is the leprosy of the Soul.

Saint John Baptist de Rossi

MAY 24

Our first aim is
to go to God;
we are not on Earth
for anything but this!

Saint John Vianney

MAY 25

Your example, even more than your words, will be an eloquent lesson to the world.

Saint Madeleine Sophie Barat

MAY 26

There is nothing more dangerous in the spiritual life, than to wish to rule ourselves after our own way of thinking.

Saint Philip Neri

MAY 27

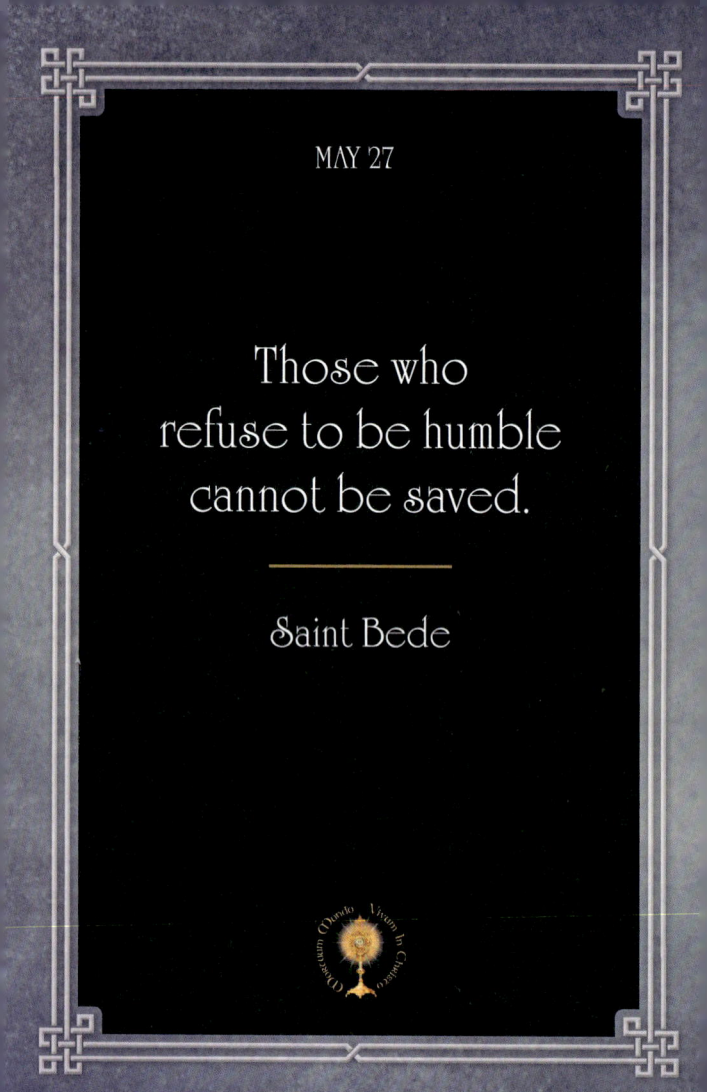

Those who refuse to be humble cannot be saved.

———

Saint Bede

MAY 28

To sacrifice what you are and to live without belief, that is a fate more terrible than dying.

―――

Saint Joan of Arc

MAY 29

Trials are nothing else but the forge that purifies the soul of all its imperfections.

―――

Saint Mary Magdalen de Pazzi

MAY 30

I would rather die, than do a thing, which I know to be a sin, or against the will of God.

Saint Joan of Arc

MAY 31

Most blessed are you among women and blessed is the fruit of your womb.

Saint Elizabeth

Dead Theologians Society became a Private Association of the Faithful in 2015.

JUNE
THE SACRED HEART OF JESUS

The Sacred Heart of Jesus
by Charles Bosseron Chambers

Wisdom & Inspiration from the Saints for

JUNE

JUNE 01

The Cross is the way to Paradise, but only when it is borne willingly.

St. Paul of the Cross

JUNE 02

You will accomplish more by kind words and a courteous manner than by anger or sharp rebuke, which should never be used except in necessity.

Saint Angela Merici

JUNE 03

A Christian who gives his life for God is not afraid to die.

———

Saint Charles Lwanga

JUNE 04

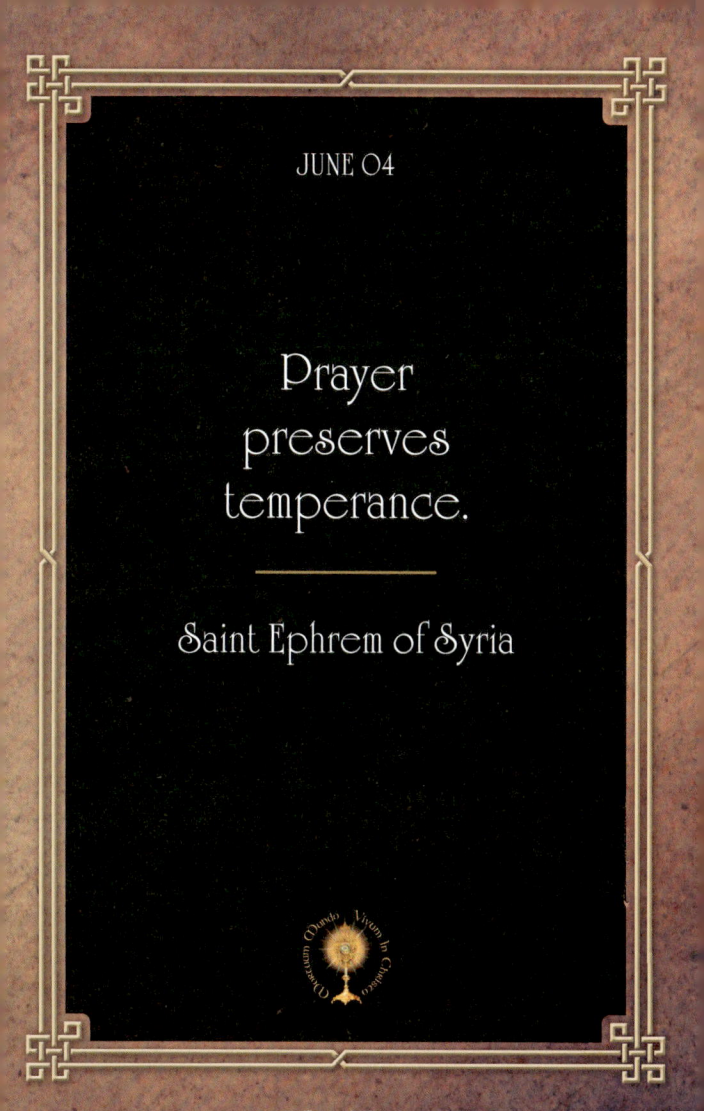

Prayer preserves temperance.

―――――

Saint Ephrem of Syria

JUNE 05

All sins are repulsive before God, but the most repulsive is pride of the heart.

Saint Anthony of Padua

JUNE 06

You will never enjoy the sweetness of a quiet prayer unless you shut your mind to all worldly desires & temporal affairs.

Saint Norbert

JUNE 07

Prayer suppresses anger.

———

Saint Ephrem of Syria

JUNE 08

Actions speak louder than words; let your words teach and your actions speak.

―――

Saint Anthony of Padua

JUNE 09

Prayer prevents emotions of pride and envy.

Saint Ephrem of Syria

JUNE 10

I thank you, Almighty God, for sending me so great a sorrow to purify me from my sins.

Saint Margaret of Scotland

JUNE 11

Without grace there is no hope, but with it there is no shortage.

———

Saint Barnabas

JUNE 12

I confess frequently because I sin frequently.

———

Saint John of Facundo

JUNE 13

The life of the body is the soul; the life of the soul is God.

———

Saint Anthony of Padua

JUNE 14

Though you speak to yourself in secret, your words are examined in Heaven.

Saint Basil the Great

JUNE 15

Don't wait until you are old to start becoming a saint.

Saint Josemaria Escriva

JUNE 16

In my opinion there is hardly anything else that the enemy of our soul [that is, Satan] dreads more than confidence – humble confidence in God.

―――――

Blessed Solanus Casey

JUNE 17

Until we have a passionate love for Our Lord in the Blessed Sacrament we shall accomplish nothing.

Saint Peter Julian Eymard

JUNE 18

Anyone who wants to be an example to others, must first examine himself.

―――

Saint Ephrem of Syria

JUNE 19

As soon as you willfully allow a dialogue with temptation to begin, the soul is robbed of peace, just as consent to impurity destroys grace.

Saint Josemaria Escriva

JUNE 20

Be not afraid;
my Immaculate Heart
will be your refuge
and your safe path
to God.

───────

Our Lady of Fatima

JUNE 21

It is better to be a child of God than king of the whole world.

———

Saint Aloysius Gonzaga

JUNE 22

Occupy your minds with good thoughts, or the enemy will fill them with bad ones.

Saint Thomas More

JUNE 23

A good man is not a perfect man; a good man is an honest man, faithful and unhesitatingly responsive to the voice of God in his life.

Saint John Fisher

JUNE 24

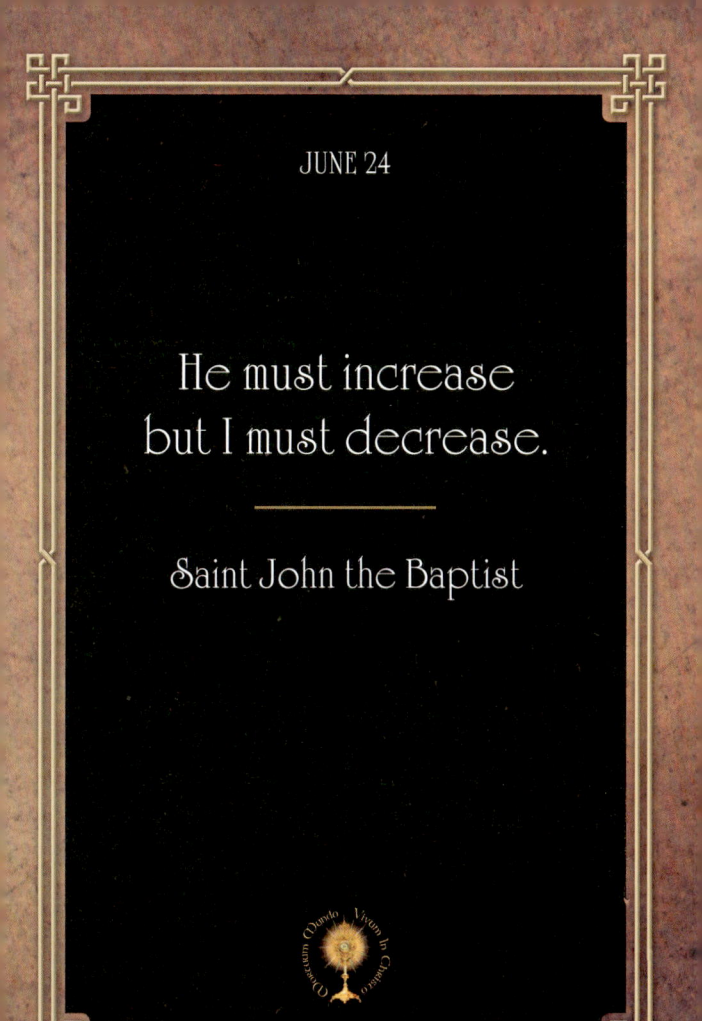

He must increase
but I must decrease.

———

Saint John the Baptist

JUNE 25

When we resolve firmly to lead a clean life, chastity will not be a burden to you: it will be a triumphant crown.

―――――

Saint Josemaria Escriva

JUNE 26

A man who fails to love the Mass fails to love Christ.

Saint Josemaria Escriva

JUNE 27

If anyone does not wish to have Mary Immaculate for his Mother, he will not have Christ as his Brother.

Saint Maximillian Kolbe

JUNE 28

The business of the Christian is nothing else but to be ever preparing for death.

Saint Irenaeus

JUNE 29

It is impossible for us not to speak about what we have seen and heard.

———

Saint Peter

JUNE 30

Bad company ruins good morals.

Saint Paul

JULY
THE PRECIOUS BLOOD OF JESUS

Christ Crucified
by Diego Velázquez (1632)

Wisdom & Inspiration from the Saints for

JULY

JULY 01

I'd rather die ten thousand deaths, than wrongfully take away one farthing of any man's goods, one day of his liberty, or one minute of his life.

Saint Oliver Plunket

JULY 02

Always forward, never back.

Saint Junipero Serra

JULY 03

Error never shows itself in its naked reality, in order not to be discovered.

Saint Irenaeus

JULY 04

If you love peace, all will be well.

Saint Elizabeth of Portugal

JULY 05

What good thing could God deny us when He is the one who invites us to ask?

Saint Anthony Mary Zaccaria

JULY 06

The Lord prefers to wait himself for the sinner for years rather than keep us waiting for an instant.

Saint Maria Goretti

JULY 07

The first step of humility is unhesitating obedience, which comes naturally to those who cherish Christ above all.

Saint Benedict

We should remember, in all the controversies in which we engage, to treat our opponents as if they were acting in good faith, even if they seem to us to be acting out of spite or self-interest.

Saint John Fisher

JULY 09

I do not care very much what men say of me, provided God approves of me.

Saint Thomas More

JULY 10

Be careful to be gentle, lest in removing the rust, you break the whole instrument.

Saint Benedict

JULY 11

Whenever a real
misfortune happens,
I am quite resigned, and
I await with confidence
the help of God.

Saint Zelie Martin

JULY 12

Soon we'll have the intimate happiness of the family, and it's this beauty that brings us closer to Him.

Saint Louis Martin

JULY 13

Be assured that you are pleasing in the sight of God and that I shall help you when I am with Him.

Saint Kateri Tekakwitha

JULY 14

If you learn
everything but Christ,
you learn nothing.

―――

Saint Bonaventure

JULY 15

If you learn nothing except Christ, you learn everything.

Saint Bonaventure

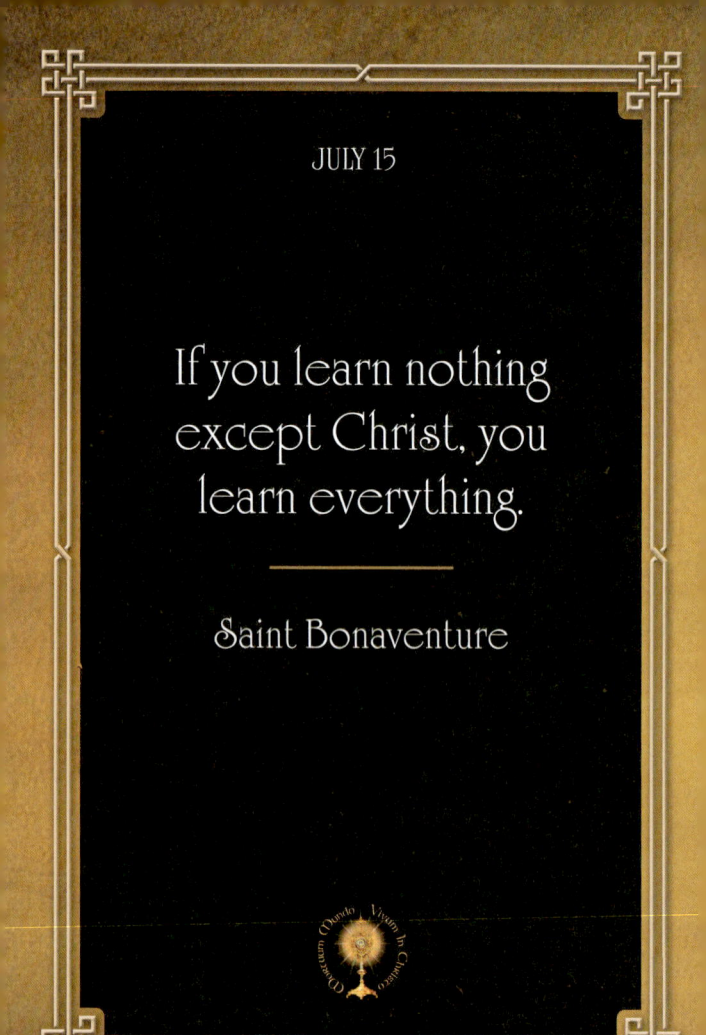

JULY 16

I am always thinking of you and helping you to secure eternal life.

Our Lady of Mount Carmel

JULY 17

I have given myself entirely to Jesus Christ and it is not possible to change masters.

Saint Kateri Tekakwitha

JULY 18

Commitment is doing what you said you would do, after the feeling you said it in has passed.

―――――

Saint Camillus de Lellis

JULY 19

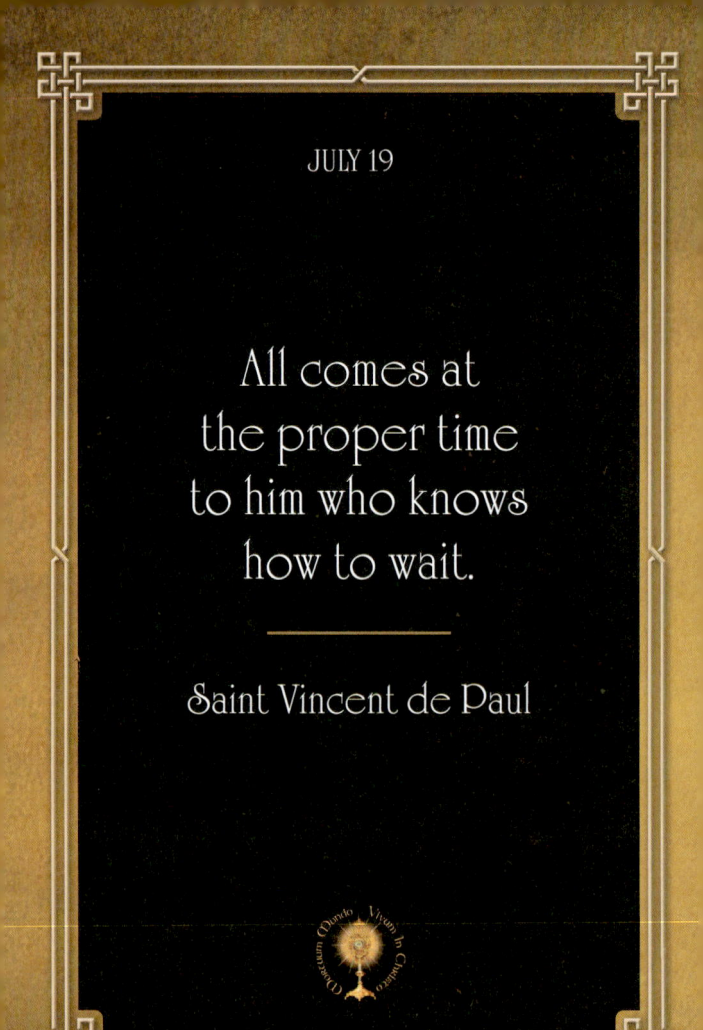

All comes at the proper time to him who knows how to wait.

Saint Vincent de Paul

JULY 20

If I do not speak the truth, I become a slave of the father of lies and become a member of this father of lies.

Saint Jerome Emiliani

JULY 21

The Holy Spirit sweetens the yoke of the divine law and lightens its weight, so that we may observe God's commandments with the greatest of ease and even with pleasure.

Saint Lawrence of Brindisi

JULY 22

We must be faithful to the present moment or we will frustrate the plan of God for our lives.

Blessed Solanus Casey

JULY 23

To write well and speak well is mere vanity if one does not live well.

Saint Bridget of Sweden

JULY 24

Arm yourselves with the Rosary, for the name of Mary dispels the darkness and crushes evil.

———

Saint Charbel Makhluf

JULY 25

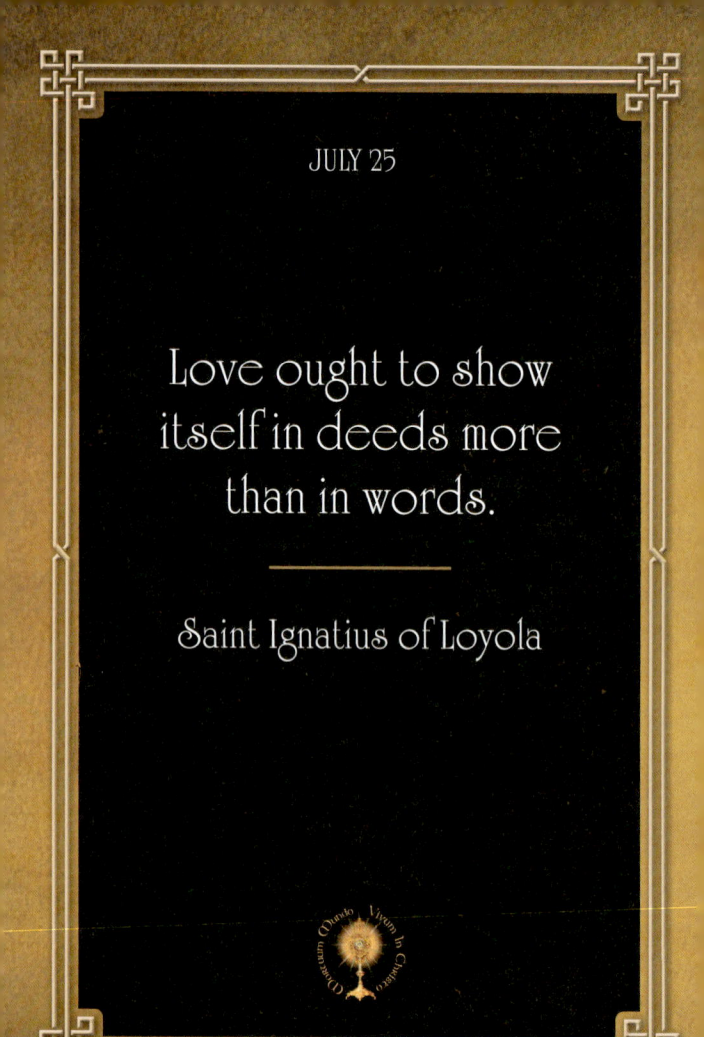

Love ought to show itself in deeds more than in words.

Saint Ignatius of Loyola

JULY 26

For he who touches the Body of Christ unworthily, receives his damnation.

Saint Peter Chrysologus

JULY 27

You wouldn't abandon ship in a storm just because you cannot control the winds.

Saint Thomas More

JULY 28

If you can honestly humble yourself, your victory is won.

Blessed Solanus Casey

JULY 29

To offend Him ought to offend us, and so we must keep sure to guard our vices of thought or hold our tongue.

Saint Benedict

JULY 30

Anyone who wishes to frolic with the devil cannot rejoice with Christ.

Saint Peter Chrysologus

JULY 31

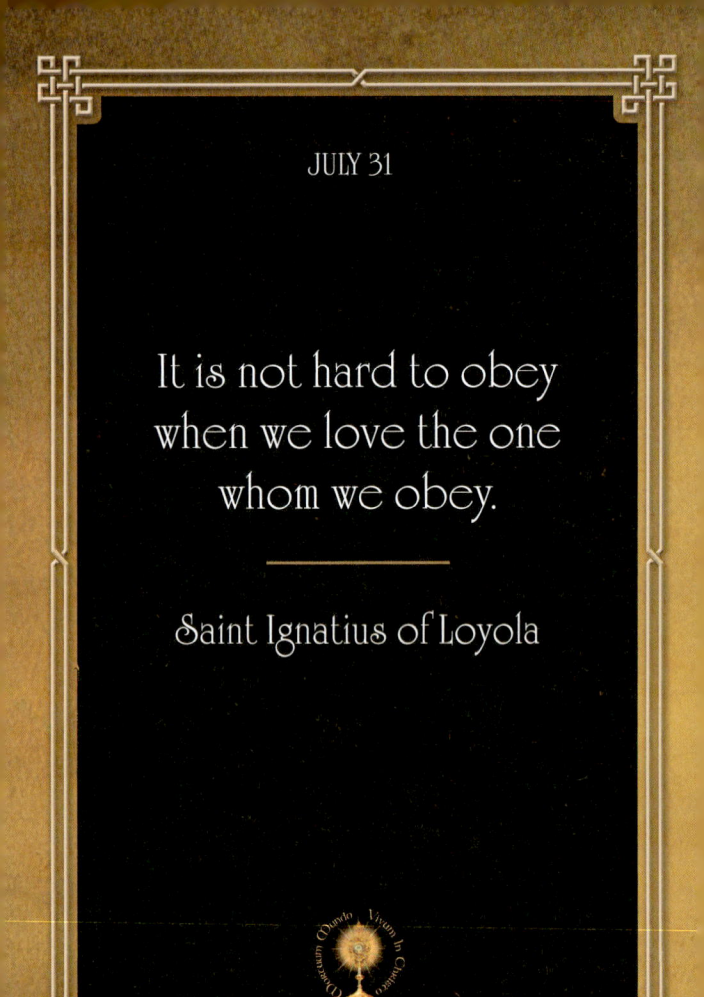

It is not hard to obey when we love the one whom we obey.

Saint Ignatius of Loyola

A special charism of
Dead Theologians Society
is to pray for souls in
purgatory.

AUGUST
THE IMMACULATE HEART OF MARY

The Immacualte Heart of Mary
by Leopold Kupelwieser

Wisdom & Inspiration from the Saints for

AUGUST

AUGUST 01

Those who say the Rosary daily and wear the Brown Scapular and who do a little more will go straight to Heaven.

Saint Alphonsus Liguori

AUGUST 02

In one day, the Eucharist will make you produce more for the glory of God than a whole lifetime without it.

Saint Peter Julian Eymard

AUGUST 03

Heretics are to be converted by an example of humility and other virtues far more readily than by any external display or verbal battles.

Saint Dominic

AUGUST 04

The man of impure speech is a person whose lips are but an opening and a supply pipe which hell uses to vomit its impurities upon the earth.

Saint John Vianney

AUGUST 05

So closely are Jesus and Mary bound up with each other that whoever beholds Jesus sees Mary; whoever loves Jesus, loves Mary; whoever has devotion to Jesus, has devotion to Mary.

Saint John Eudes

AUGUST 06

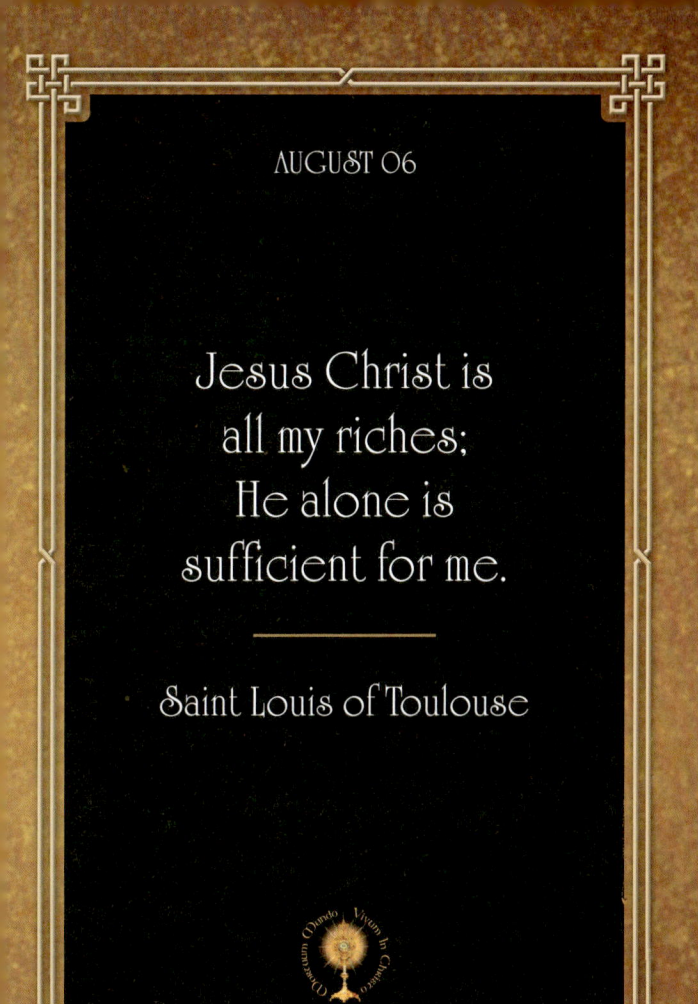

Jesus Christ is all my riches; He alone is sufficient for me.

Saint Louis of Toulouse

AUGUST 07

Do not receive Christ in the Blessed Sacrament so that you may use Him as you judge best but give yourself to Him and let Him receive you in this Sacrament so that He Himself, God your Savior may do to you and through you whatever He wills.

Saint Cajetan

AUGUST 08

I am not capable of doing big things, but I want to do everything, even the smallest things for the greater glory of God.

Saint Dominic

AUGUST 09

Since Mary is the prototype of pure womanhood, the imitation of Mary must be the goal of girls' education.

Saint Edith Stein

AUGUST 10

Sheltered under the name of Jesus Christ, I do not fear these pains, for they do not last long.

Saint Lawrence

AUGUST 11

We become what we love and who we love shapes what we become.

Saint Clare of Assisi

AUGUST 12

Suffering borne in the will quietly and patiently is a continual, very powerful prayer before God.

———

Saint Jane Frances de Chantal

AUGUST 13

Torture as much as thou pleases, still shall I proclaim myself a Christian.

Saint Euplius

AUGUST 14

When you kneel before an altar, do it in such a way that others may be able to recognize that you know before whom you kneel.

Saint Maximilian Kolbe

AUGUST 15

If there were one million families praying the Rosary every day, the entire world would be saved.

Pope Saint Pius X

AUGUST 16

Be humble in
this life, that God
may raise you up
in the next.

———

Saint Stephen of Hungary

AUGUST 17

The gift of grace increases as the struggle increases.

Saint Rose of Lima

AUGUST 18

Misfortune is more useful to the friends of God than good fortune, for on such occasions they can prove their loyalty to their Lord.

Saint Louis of Toulouse

AUGUST 19

Every Saint belongs to the court of the Queen of All Saints.

———

Saint John Eudes

AUGUST 20

The eyes have wandered and the mind soon follows.

Saint Bernard of Clairvaux

AUGUST 21

All the strength of Satan's reign is due to the easy-going weakness of Catholics.

Pope Saint Pius X

AUGUST 22

Faith is to believe what you do not see; the reward of faith is to see what you believe.

Saint Augustine

AUGUST 23

Know that the greatest service that man can offer God is to help convert souls.

Saint Rose of Lima

AUGUST 24

Once you begin to believe there is help out there, you will know it to be true.

Saint Bartholomew

AUGUST 25

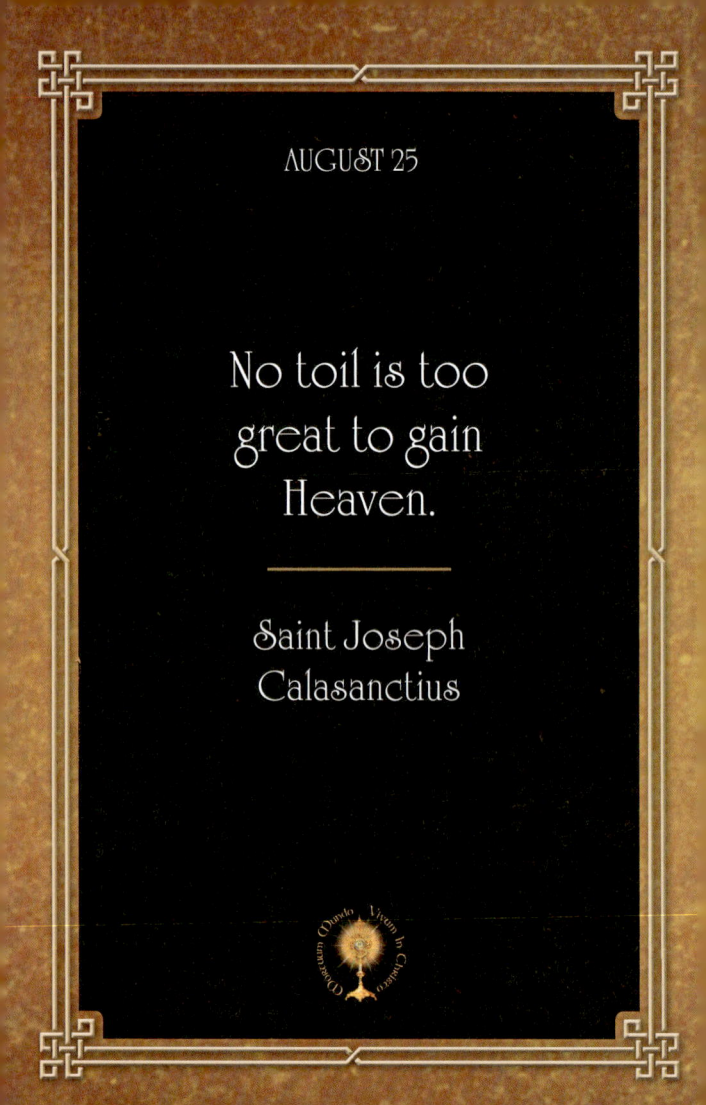

No toil is too great to gain Heaven.

Saint Joseph Calasanctius

AUGUST 26

Do not pray for easy lives, pray to be stronger.

Blessed Solanus Casey

AUGUST 27

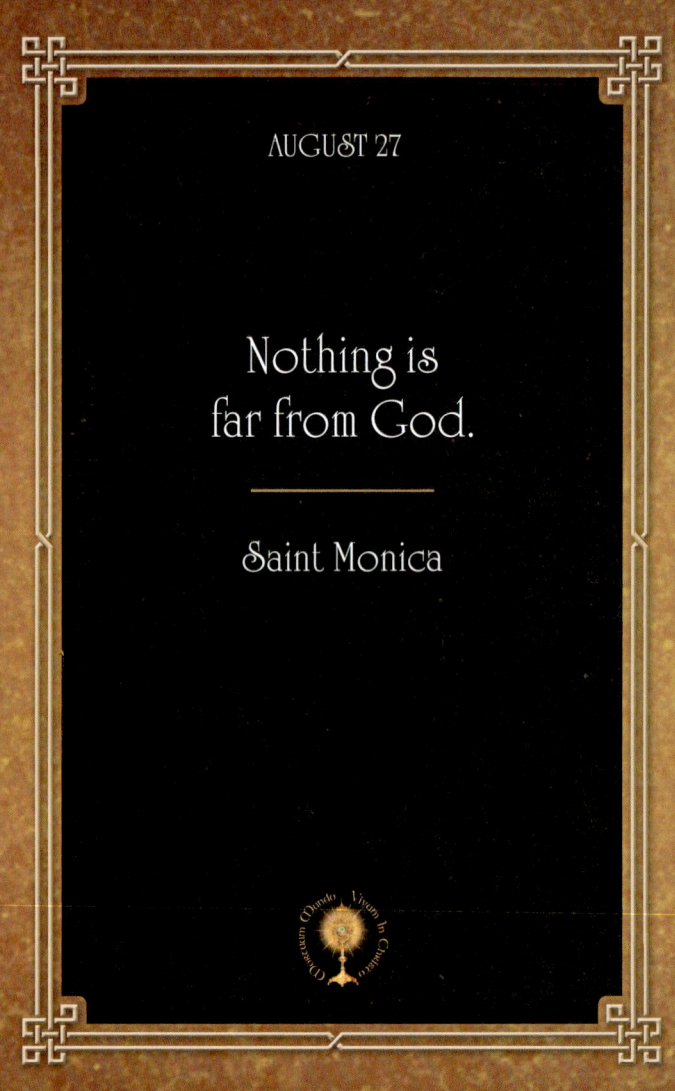

Nothing is far from God.

Saint Monica

AUGUST 28

Take care of your body as if you were going to live forever, and take care of your Soul as if you were going to die tomorrow.

Saint Augustine

AUGUST 29

Ah, my dear Lord, what melancholy company is that person who is a slave to anger!

Saint John Vianney

AUGUST 30

Apart from the cross there is no other ladder by which we may get to Heaven.

Saint Rose of Lima

AUGUST 31

A man who governs his passions is master of the world.

———

Saint Dominic

The Motto for
Dead Theologians Society
is "Dead to the World –
Alive in Christ!"

SEPTEMBER
THE SEVEN SORROWS OF MARY

The Madonna in Sorrow
Sassoferrato

Wisdom & Inspiration from the Saints for

SEPTEMBER

SEPTEMBER 01

The body was made for the soul, and this world for the sake of the other world.

Saint Giles

SEPTEMBER 02

The Church alone, being the Bride of Christ, and having all things in common with her Divine Spouse, is the depository of the Truth.

Pope Saint Pius X

SEPTEMBER 03

The proof of love is in the works.

Saint Gregory the Great

SEPTEMBER 04

For those who live well in the world, death is not frightening, but sweet and precious.

———

Saint Rose of Viterbo

SEPTEMBER 05

If you judge people, you have no time to love them.

Saint Teresa of Calcutta

SEPTEMBER 06

Consider the end of life and you will love nothing of this world.

Saint Lawrence Justinian

SEPTEMBER 07

The love of husband and wife is the force that welds society together.

Saint John Chrysostom

SEPTEMBER 08

The Mighty One has done great things for me, and holy is His name.

Blessed Virgin Mary

SEPTEMBER 09

We must speak to them with our hands before we speak to them with our lips.

Saint Peter Claver

SEPTEMBER 10

Keep close to the Catholic Church at all times, for the Church alone can give you true peace, since she alone possesses Jesus, the true Prince of Peace, in the Blessed Sacrament.

Saint Padre Pio

SEPTEMBER 11

If the world could see the beauty of a soul without sin, all sinners, all non-believers would instantly convert their lives.

Saint Padre Pio

SEPTEMBER 12

We must continue to do good, even though people of the world may criticize us.

Saint Vincent de Paul

SEPTEMBER 13

Slander is worse than cannibalism.

Saint John Chrysostom

SEPTEMBER 14

We are Christians only is so far as we believe in Jesus and keep His word.

Blessed Solanus Casey

SEPTEMBER 15

Any time spent before the Eucharistic presence, be it long or short, is the best-spent time of our lives.

Saint Catherine of Genoa

SEPTEMBER 16

Above all everyone in conversation should try to avoid anger or bad temper, or showing he is annoyed with someone, and no one should hurt another in word or deed, or in any way.

Saint Vincent de Paul

SEPTEMBER 17

The Rosary is the 'weapon' for these times.

Saint Padre Pio

SEPTEMBER 18

The soul suffers whenever the flesh rejoices in sinning.

Saint Hildegard of Bingen

SEPTEMBER 19

When you don't have time, at least say an 'Our Father' and a 'Hail Mary', but when you can, say more.

Our Lady of La Salette

SEPTEMBER 20

It is a most grievous sin for people united in matrimony and blessed with children to neglect their children or their good upbringing, or to allow them to lack the necessities of life.

Saint Robert Bellarmine

SEPTEMBER 21

Beware of angling for compliments, lest you lose God's favor in exchange for people's praise.

Saint Jerome

SEPTEMBER 22

Charity is not just giving, rather removing the need of those who receive charity and liberating them from it.

Saint Thomas of Villanova

SEPTEMBER 23

Remember, the Devil has only one door with which to enter into our soul: our will.

Saint Padre Pio

SEPTEMBER 24

We ought, you see my dear brethren, to have a great respect for the name of God and pronounce it only with tremendous veneration and never in vain.

Saint John Vianney

SEPTEMBER 25

Pride could not last even for a moment in Heaven, nor will it ever be able to get close to it.

Saint Elizabeth of Schonau

SEPTEMBER 26

Our single endeavor should be to give ourselves to the work and to be faithful to Him, and not to spoil His work by our shortcomings.

Saint Isaac Jogues

SEPTEMBER 27

As soon as
we empty ourselves
of self, God will fill
us with Himself.

Saint Vincent de Paul

SEPTEMBER 28

I am a Catholic and wholeheartedly do accept death for God; had I a thousand lives, all these to Him shall I offer.

Saint Lawrence Ruiz

SEPTEMBER 29

Always stay close to this Heavenly Mother, because She is the sea to be crossed to reach the shores of Eternal splendor.

Saint Padre Pio

SEPTEMBER 30

Ignorance of the Scriptures is ignorance of Christ.

Saint Jerome

OCTOBER
OUR LADY OF THE ROSARY

Our Lady of the Rosary
by Charles Bosseron Chambers

Wisdom & Inspiration from the Saints for

OCTOBER

OCTOBER 01

A word or a smile is often enough to put fresh life in a despondent soul.

———

Saint Thérèse of Lisieux

OCTOBER 02

How happy are they who have no other obligation but to praise the Lord night and day, and who live always in His presence.

Saint Gerard of Brogne

OCTOBER 03

Patience obtains all things.

Saint Teresa of Jesus
(Teresa of Ávila)

OCTOBER 04

It is not fitting, when one is in God's service, to have a gloomy face or a chilling look.

Saint Francis of Assisi

OCTOBER 05

If the angels were capable of envy, they would envy us for two things: one is receiving Holy Communion, and the other is suffering.

Saint Faustina Kowalska

OCTOBER 06

While the world changes, the Cross stands firm.

———

Saint Bruno

OCTOBER 07

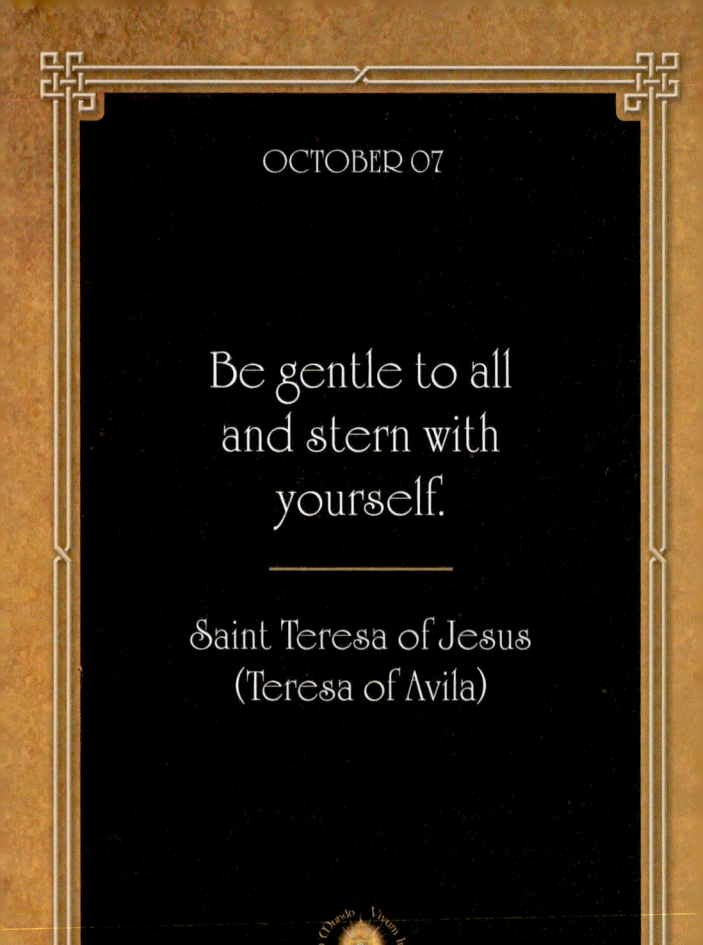

Be gentle to all and stern with yourself.

Saint Teresa of Jesus
(Teresa of Avila)

OCTOBER 08

I have nothing left, but I still have my heart, and with that I can always love.

Blessed Chiara Luce Badano

OCTOBER 09

Those who want to work for moral reform in the world must seek the glory of God before all else.

Saint John Leonardi

OCTOBER 10

I have great doubts about the salvation of those who do not have special devotion to Mary.

Saint Francis Borgia

OCTOBER 11

A peaceful man does more good than a learned one.

———

Pope Saint John XXIII

OCTOBER 12

The Eucharist
is the highway
to heaven.

―――――

Blessed Carlo Acutis

OCTOBER 13

Departing from the land of the dying, I hope to see the good things of the Lord in the land of the living.

Saint Edward
the Confessor

OCTOBER 14

It is the duty of every man to uphold the dignity of every woman.

Pope Saint John Paul II

OCTOBER 15

When the devil reminds you of your past, remind him of his future.

———

Saint Teresa of Jesus
(Teresa of Avila)

OCTOBER 16

Consider the shortness of time, the length of eternity and reflect how everything here below comes to an end and passes by.

Saint Gerard Majella

OCTOBER 17

Be careful, therefore, to take part only in the one Eucharist; for there is only one Flesh of our Lord Jesus Christ and one cup to unite us with His blood.

Saint Ignatius of Antioch

OCTOBER 18

A person's rightful due is to be treated as an object of love, not as an object of use.

Pope Saint John Paul II

OCTOBER 19

Truly, matters in the world are in a bad state; but if you and I begin in earnest to reform ourselves, a really good beginning will have been made.

Saint Peter of Alcantara

OCTOBER 20

When you feel the assaults of passion and anger, then it is time to be silent as Jesus was silent in the midst of His ignominies and sufferings.

Saint Paul of the Cross

OCTOBER 21

Fight all error but do it with humor, patience, kindness and love.

Saint John of Kanty

OCTOBER 22

Freedom consists not in doing what we like, but in having the right to do what we ought.

Pope Saint John Paul II

OCTOBER 23

Although the sinner does not believe in Hell, he shall nevertheless go there if he has the misfortune to die in mortal sin.

Saint Anthony Mary Claret

OCTOBER 24

When people love and recite the Rosary, they find it makes them better.

Saint Anthony Mary Claret

OCTOBER 25

Atheism robs man
of supernatural hope
— the very soul
of happiness.

Blessed Solanus Casey

OCTOBER 26

To save the souls of poor sinners, God wishes to establish the devotion to my Immaculate Heart throughout the world.

Our Lady of Fatima

OCTOBER 27

I will be kind to everybody, particularly to those whom I find troublesome.

Saint Anthony Mary Claret

OCTOBER 28

Every part of the journey is of importance to the whole.

―――――

Saint Teresa of Jesus
(Teresa of Avila)

OCTOBER 29

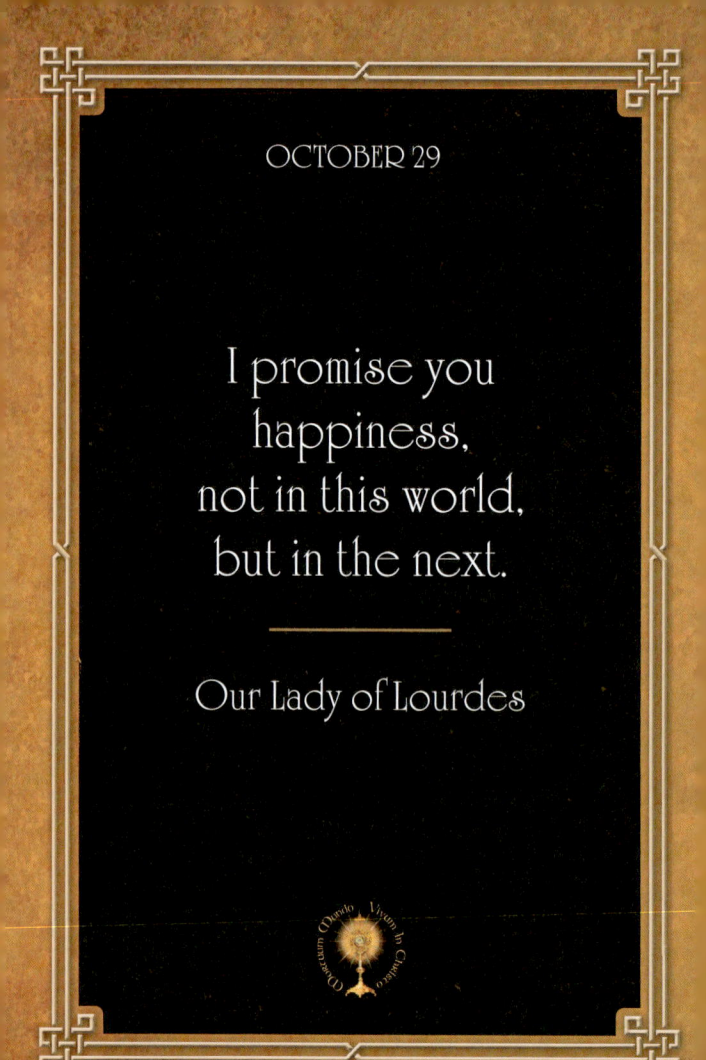

I promise you happiness, not in this world, but in the next.

Our Lady of Lourdes

OCTOBER 30

It is a common teaching of the Saints that one of the principal means of leading a good and exemplary life is certainly modesty and the mortification of the eyes.

———

Saint Alphonsus Rodriquez

OCTOBER 31

A soul in the state of grace need fear nothing from devils, for they are so cowardly that they flee from the gaze of a child.

Saint Thérèse of Lisieux

The Prayer of St. Gertrude

Eternal Father, I offer Thee the Most Precious Blood of Thy Divine Son, Jesus, in union with the masses said throughout the world today, for all the holy souls in purgatory, for sinners everywhere, for sinners in the universal church, those in my own home and within my family.

Amen

NOVEMBER
PURGATORY

Souls in Purgatory
Philippe de Champaigne

Wisdom & Inspiration from the Saints for

NOVEMBER

NOVEMBER 01

Let us become Saints so that after having been together on Earth, we may be together in Heaven.

Saint Padre Pio

NOVEMBER 02

In our prayers, let us not forget sinners and the poor souls in Purgatory, especially our poor relatives.

Saint Bernadette Soubirous

NOVEMBER 03

Everything, even sweeping, scraping vegetables, weeding a garden and waiting on the sick could be a prayer, if it were offered to God.

Saint Martin de Porres

NOVEMBER 04

Be sure that
you first preach by
the way you live.

Saint Charles Borromeo

NOVEMBER 05

I have neither permitted, nor shall I permit, the things that have been settled by the holy fathers to be violated by any innovation.

Saint Leo the Great

NOVEMBER 06

Property –
the more common it becomes the more holy it becomes.

Saint Gertrude the Great

NOVEMBER 07

A soul that has never tasted the sweetness of inner silence is a restless spirit which disturbs the silence of others.

Saint Faustina Kowalska

NOVEMBER 08

If you think someone is not worthy of your mercy, you should realize that you don't deserve mercy either.

Saint Josemaria Escriva

NOVEMBER 09

It is a great wisdom to know how to be silent and to look at neither the remarks, nor the deeds, nor the lives of others.

Saint John of the Cross

NOVEMBER 10

Virtue is nothing without the trial of temptation, for there is no conflict without an enemy, no victory without strife.

Saint Leo the Great

NOVEMBER 11

Lord, if your people need me, I will not refuse to serve.

Saint Martin of Tours

NOVEMBER 12

Lord, grant me the grace to shed my blood for the unity of the Church and in behalf of obedience to the Holy See.

Saint Josaphat

NOVEMBER 13

The world is poisoned by erroneous theories, and needs to be taught sane doctrines, but it is difficult to straighten what has become crooked.

Saint Frances Xavier Cabrini

NOVEMBER 14

The world would have peace if only the men of politics would follow the Gospels.

———

Saint Bridget of Sweden

NOVEMBER 15

The greater and more persistent your confidence in God, the more abundantly you will receive what you ask.

───────

Saint Albert the Great

NOVEMBER 16

Every time we look at the Blessed Sacrament our place in Heaven is raised forever.

Saint Gertrude the Great

NOVEMBER 17

Have a great love
for those who contradict
and fail to love you, for
in this way love is
begotten in a heart
that has no love.

———

Saint John of the Cross

NOVEMBER 18

There are no difficulties except for those who worry too much about tomorrow.

Saint Rose Philippine Duchesne

NOVEMBER 19

It is not the bad thought, but the consent to it, that is sinful.

Saint Alphonsus Liguori

NOVEMBER 20

Before you receive Jesus Christ, you should remove from your heart all worldly attachments which you know to be displeasing to Him.

Saint Augustine

NOVEMBER 21

At this point I have nothing left, but I still have my heart, and with that I can always love.

Blessed Chiara
Luce Badano

NOVEMBER 22

Yelling and shouting is what idiots do.

Saint Clement of Alexandria

NOVEMBER 23

Long live Christ the King!

Blessed Miguel Pro

NOVEMBER 24

A Christian should always remember that the value of his good works is not based on their number and excellence, but on the love of God which prompts him to do these things.

Saint John of the Cross

NOVEMBER 25

God, who loves tiny beginnings, will know as He always does know, how and when to provide developments.

Blessed Solanus Casey

NOVEMBER 26

What we really are consists in what God knows us to be.

Saint John Berchmans

NOVEMBER 27

If, during life, we have been kind to the suffering souls in Purgatory, God will see that help be not denied us after death.

Saint Paul of the Cross

NOVEMBER 28

One must see
God in everyone.

———

Saint Catherine Laboure

NOVEMBER 29

For those who have sinned grievously, there is no means of salvation but the confession of their sins.

Saint Alphonsus Liguori

NOVEMBER 30

Let us not hesitate to help those who have died and to offer our prayers for them.

Saint John Chrysostom

DECEMBER
THE IMMACULATE CONCEPTION

The Immaculate Conception
by Bartolomé Esteban Murillo (c1678)

Wisdom & Inspiration from the Saints for

DECEMBER

DECEMBER 01

To be a Catholic
is my greatest glory.

Saint Edmund Campion

DECEMBER 02

Consider that although we may reckon ourselves to be righteous and frequently succeed in deceiving men, we can conceal nothing from God.

Saint Nicholas

DECEMBER 03

Many, many people hereabouts are not becoming Christians for one reason only; there is nobody to make them Christians.

Saint Francis Xavier

DECEMBER 04

Let us carefully observe the manner of life of all the apostles, martyrs, ascetics and just men who announce the coming of the Lord.

Saint John Damascene

DECEMBER 05

Pray, pray a great deal and make many sacrifices, for many souls go to Hell because they have no one to make sacrifices and pray for them.

Our Lady of Fatima

DECEMBER 06

Let us therefore strive to preserve the holiness of our souls and to guard the purity of our bodies with all fervor.

———

Saint Nicholas

DECEMBER 07

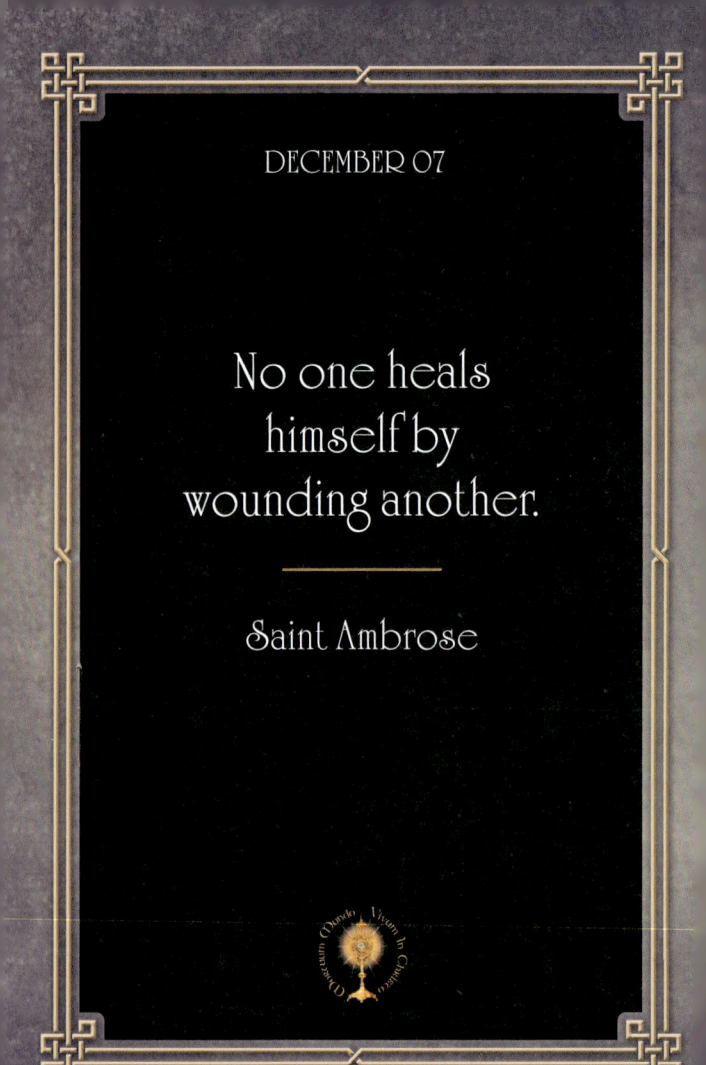

No one heals himself by wounding another.

Saint Ambrose

DECEMBER 08

I come to tell you that they suffer in Purgatory, that they weep, and that they demand with urgent cries the help of your prayers and your good works.

Saint John Vianney

DECEMBER 09

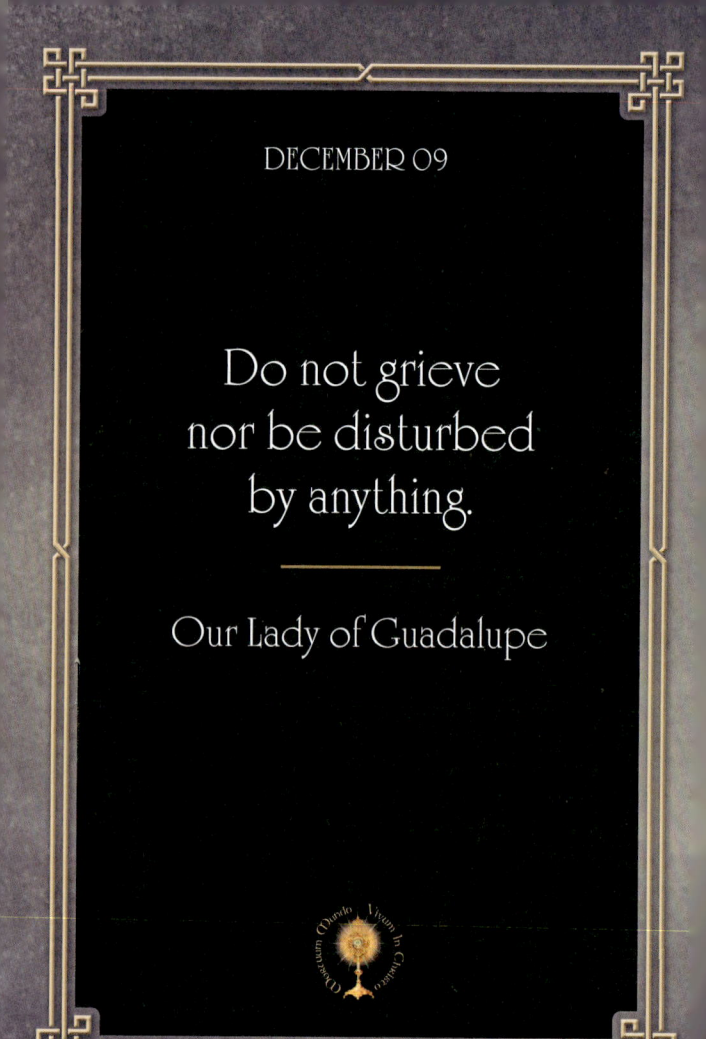

Do not grieve nor be disturbed by anything.

Our Lady of Guadalupe

DECEMBER 10

Those whose hearts are pure are temples of the Holy Spirit.

Saint Lucy

DECEMBER 11

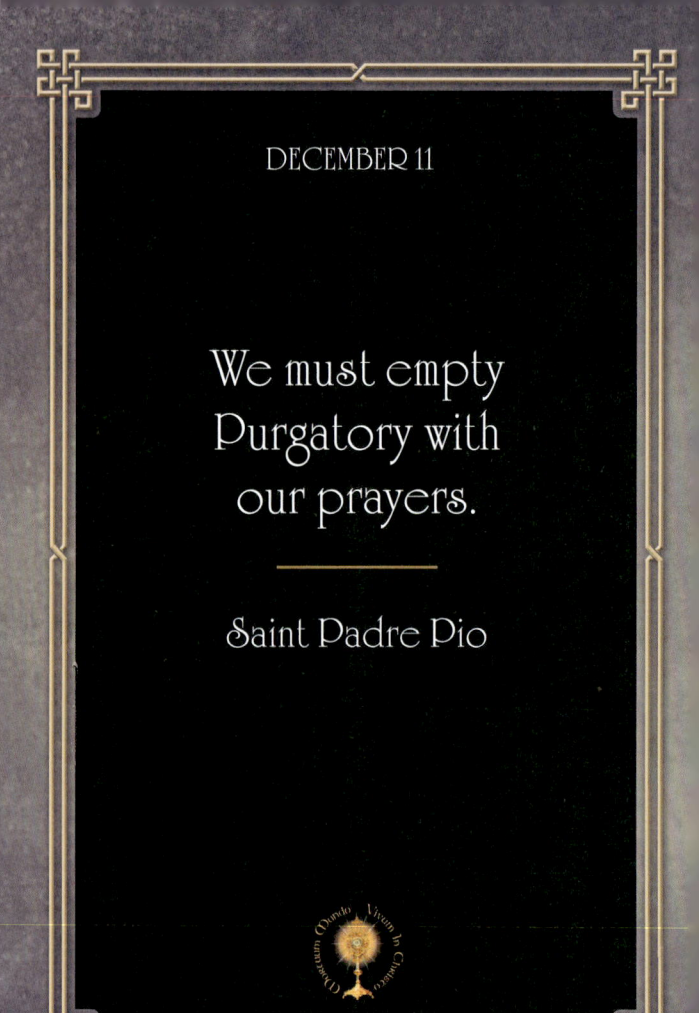

We must empty Purgatory with our prayers.

Saint Padre Pio

DECEMBER 12

To live without faith, without a heritage to defend, without battling constantly for truth, is not to live but to 'get along'; we must never just 'get along'.

Blessed Pier Giorgio Frassati

DECEMBER 13

No one's body is polluted so as to endanger the soul if it has not pleased the mind.

Saint Lucy

DECEMBER 14

In sorrow and suffering, go straight to God with confidence, and you will be strengthened, enlightened and instructed.

Saint John of the Cross

DECEMBER 15

This is the Bread of everlasting life which supports the substance of our soul.

———

Saint Ambrose

DECEMBER 16

Apart from the Cross, there is no other ladder by which we may get to Heaven.

Saint Rose of Lima

DECEMBER 17

The Lord opened the understanding of my unbelieving heart, so that I should recall my sins.

—

Saint Patrick

DECEMBER 18

Teach us to
give and not count
the cost.

———

Saint Ignatius of Loyola

DECEMBER 19

Our hearts are made for You, O Lord, and they are restless until they rest in You.

Saint Augustine

DECEMBER 20

When something distasteful and unpleasant comes your way, remember Christ crucified and be silent.

———

Saint John of the Cross

DECEMBER 21

If you have too much to do, with God's help you will find time to do it all.

Saint Peter Canisius

DECEMBER 22

I will go anywhere and do anything in order to communicate the love of Jesus to those who do not know Him or have forgotten Him.

Saint Frances Xavier Cabrini

DECEMBER 23

You cannot be half a saint; you must be a whole saint or no saint at all.

———

Saint Thérèse of Lisieux

DECEMBER 24

Charity is that with which no man is lost, and without which no man is saved.

Saint Robert Bellarmine

DECEMBER 25

It is Christmas, every time you let God love others through you.

Saint Teresa of Calcutta

DECEMBER 26

Remember the Christian life is one of action; not of speech and daydreams.

———

Saint Vincent Pallotti

DECEMBER 27

Devote one hour daily to mental prayer – if you can, let it be early in the morning, because then your mind is less cumbered and more vigorous after the night's rest.

───────

Saint Francis de Sales

DECEMBER 28

He who rejoices at the fall of another rejoices at the victory of the devil.

Saint Ambrose

DECEMBER 29

Let it be your consolation, then, that God's enemies, however honorable and exalted they may have been, shall nevertheless fade away like the smoke.

Saint Thomas Becket

DECEMBER 30

May all Christians be found worthy of either the pure white crown of a holy life or the royal red crown of martyrdom.

Saint Cyprian

DECEMBER 31

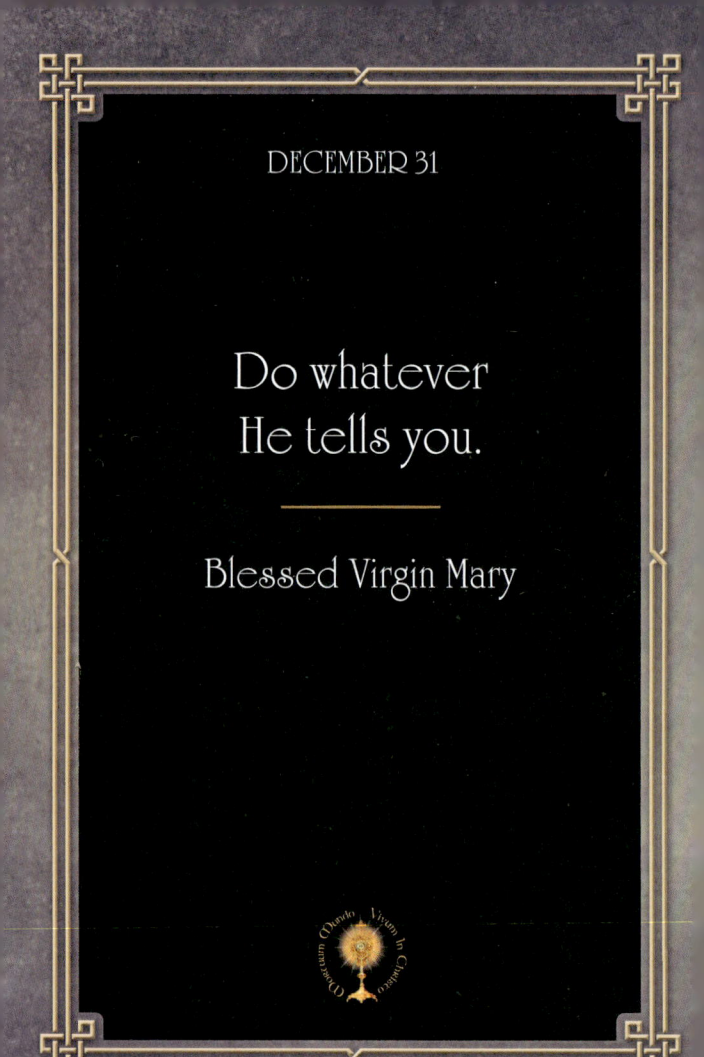

Do whatever
He tells you.

Blessed Virgin Mary